"A unique grief story about loving a brother who chose a risk-filled passionate life, who traded comfort for peak experience, and lost his life in the bargain. A masterful guide to loving and losing the extraordinary among us."

MARY E. PLOUFFE PHD,

AUTHOR OF *I KNOW IT IN MY HEART: WALKING THROUGH GRIEF WITH A CHILD*

"Grief experts categorize those of us who have lost siblings as 'forgotten mourners,' and society does not recognize the death of a brother or sister as a major loss. Anne Pinkerton challenges such misconceptions by bringing her brother David and the pain of his death to the page, illuminating just how enormous this loss is."

ANN HOOD, AUTHOR OF *COMFORT: A JOURNEY THROUGH GRIEF*

"With the energy, skill, muscle, and bravery that powered her beloved late brother as an elite extreme adventurer, Anne Pinkerton's *Were You Close?* is as much map as memoir, illustrating how the author scaled her personal mountain range of grief. Her precisely detailed example of turning to, rather than from, the facts and pain of a loved one's death is a path to emulate, especially in a culture that discourages looking into the fire of heartbreak. Those whose lives continue on without their own North Stars, and all who appreciate wise and honest writing, will discover here a new author to follow anywhere."

SUZANNE STREMPEK SHEA,

AUTHOR OF *SONGS FROM A LEAD-LINED ROOM: NOTES—HIGH AND LOW—FROM MY JOURNEY THROUGH BREAST CANCER AND RADIATION*

"A heartfelt exploration of risk, loss, and self-discovery in the aftermath of tragedy. Pinkerton's generous memoir shines a necessary light on the hard road to writing about the death of a beloved sibling."

JESSICA HANDLER,

AUTHOR OF *THE MAGNETIC GIRL, INVISIBLE SISTERS, AND BRAVING THE FIRE*

"Anne Pinkerton is the real deal—an honest, unflinching memoirist who illuminates the dark corners of grief and reminds us that singular pain is often universal, can stretch across cultures, time periods, circumstances. With breathtaking detail and subtle, layered scenes, Anne guides readers through her complex and beautiful relationship with her larger-than-life adventurist older brother, David, asking us to linger in difficult, unanswerable questions about family, loss, and perseverance. That to me is the mark of a true memoirist—a writer who doesn't write to find absolute answers but to articulate deeper questions."

ANTHONY D'ARIES, AUTHOR OF *THE LANGUAGE OF MEN: A MEMOIR*

"This is a memoir, but also a book that I believe has a chance to change the lives and sorrow of anyone who enters."

MEL ALLEN, EDITOR, *YANKEE MAGAZINE*

"In her achingly candid debut memoir, *Were You Close?*, Anne Pinkerton chronicles her obsession to understand the passion that propelled her brother David, an elite climber and adventurer, into a world of risk that ultimately killed him. Her quest to unravel the strands of David's story and weave them into her own leads Pinkerton to enter and inhabit the enormity of her grief, but gifts her, too, with the soothing balm of deeper connection. Written with the tenderness and reverence only a little sister can carry for her beloved big brother, *Were You Close?* posits an alternative to the societal expectation of leaving grief somewhere on the road behind us and shows, instead, that holding it close can sometimes clear the path forward."

MELANIE BROOKS, AUTHOR OF *WRITING HARD STORIES: CELEBRATED MEMOIRISTS WHO SHAPED ART FROM TRAUMA*

"Grief is big and wild and forever shape-shifting within us. Anne Pinkerton gets that. Her memoir gives voice to a forgotten grief and reveals how those who lose a sibling are forced, again and again, to justify their heartache. *Were You Close?* captures how the death of a loved one causes us to reflect on and reassess our relationships—especially our relationship with the person who died. It is lyrical, accessible, and a necessary contribution to the literature of loss."

GABRIELLE BIRKNER, CO-AUTHOR, *MODERN LOSS: CANDID CONVERSATION ABOUT GRIEF. BEGINNERS WELCOME*

About the Author

Anne Pinkerton is a poet, essayist, and memoirist. Her work has appeared in *Hippocampus Magazine, Ars Medica, Modern Loss,* "Beautiful Things" at *River Teeth Journal, Stone Gathering,* and other journals, as well as the anthologies, *The Pandemic Midlife Crisis: Gen X Women on the Brink* and *Nothing Divine Dies: A Poetry Anthology About Nature.*

Pinkerton holds an MFA in creative nonfiction from Bay Path University and studied poetry as an undergraduate at Hampshire College. She grew up in Texas and lives in Western Massachusetts with an array of cats and dogs.

Learn more at *annepinkertonwriter.com.*

Anne Pinkerton

Were You Close?

a sister's quest
to know the
brother she lost

www.vineleavespress.com

Cover design by Jessica Bell
Interior design by Amie McCracken

For my brother David.
It was an honor to be your little sister. I'll always be grateful for
everything you taught me.

*"A mountain keeps an echo deep inside itself—
that's how I hold your voice."*
Rumi

Author's Note

Memory is a capricious thing—by definition fickle and flawed— and memoirs are named such for this reason. Grief and time mess with remembering as much as anything. This is not a book of documentary journalism, but it's the truest story I could write.

When I could, I researched and asked a lot of questions. Other times, I had to trust that I'd at least captured the essence of what happened, acknowledging that what we remember and how we remember is often as meaningful as anything else. Sometimes, that tells a truth as significant as any other.

I'm sure others experienced the same events differently. I welcome their telling.

No one but me is responsible for what is written here. Know I hit the marks the best I could.

"Were You Close?"

This is the question that people ask me when they learn that my big brother died.

Were we close?

Of course we were! That's a ridiculous question. This is David we're talking about. Not just any brother, not just anyone, the best. When I was little, he changed my diapers and made up hilarious stories to send me off to sleep. He helped me learn how to swim and ride a bike and water ski. He encouraged me to be myself no matter what anyone else thought. And he always, always put his arm around me and kissed me right on the lips whenever I saw him. I loved him tremendously, and he would have done absolutely anything for me. I feel like half a person now that he's gone. We were close.

After I stop shouting all of this in my head, my mind flashes to how much time often passed between our phone calls, how brief our emails were, how infrequently I visited him in Texas where we grew up and where he stayed, how over the course of nearly twenty years, he visited me only twice in my adopted state of Massachusetts. I didn't know what was going on in his life a lot of the time other than the major stuff, like the woman he was currently dating or which adventure race he and his team were competing in next. With shame, I remember again—for the millionth time—that I hadn't even known he was on one of his big outdoor excursions when he went missing, when it took two days to find him, when it was the end.

And after a pause, I answer softly, feeling almost embarrassed—like I'm not telling the whole truth—"Yes, yes we were."

"Were you close?"

Asked sincerely and in the spirit of comfort by so many after David's death, this question always put me on edge. It felt as though the response I gave would inform their reaction, as if what they actually wanted to ask was, "How sad are you? Do we need to brace ourselves? Or will simply saying, 'Sorry for your loss,' be sufficient?" Each time the question was posed, even if I didn't fall apart, I sensed I had to defend my grief, my shattering sense of loss; as if I had to assure the questioner that I was entitled to my bottomless sorrow and reveal how much the event blew up my family, destroyed my assumptions about the future, and tipped my whole universe on its side. There were moments I was nearly inclined to embellish reality to justify my feelings. But then I wondered at my defensiveness. Why did I have to prove anything to anyone?

"Were you close?"

Such a seemingly innocuous thing to ask with such substantial implications. How do you even define closeness? The phrasing sounds so literal, as if the inquirer is asking whether I was physically proximate to my brother. And because the geographic distance was expansive between us, that alone causes me to question myself.

Obviously, the kind of closeness that friends and colleagues wondered about in the early aftermath of David's death is emotional, experiential, intangible. It's true that I adored David, was grateful for our relationship, looked up to him during childhood, and admired him in adulthood even when I was often mystified by his desire to challenge himself athletically in difficult, even severe, ways. All I ever wanted was to understand the things he was passionate about and maybe to feel that I was equal to him in some way—not competitively, but as peers—even if it meant just finally buying him a beer, instead of him saying, "Your money's no good here," which was his way of feeling good, of taking care of a little sister the way a big brother should, like he always did, pushing a pint in front of me at the bar.

"Were you close?"

I mean, I was only his sister. Not like a wife or child or even our mother.

Mom and I found my letters to him after he died, the ones I had written through college and beyond, organized in a manila file folder in his home office filing cabinet. I was touched to see they had been preserved, but sad by what they communicated. Over and over, I had written about wanting to be with him. Over and over, I offered to take him to dinner or buy him a drink or have him stay at my house. Over and over, I asked him to visit me, pointing out all the local natural features and attractions where my husband and I lived, the ones that might have enticed him: the bike path, the mountain range, the river, the swimming holes, the gorge.

There are outdoor opportunities here too—things you would love! I wrote again and again.

And he would write back, *Sure, darlin', someday I'll come.*

So, I did pine for that kind of closeness with him—in my physical life—as well as any and every other kind of closeness. Knowing none of it could happen now not only filled my eyes with tears, the impossibility filled me with rage—for our mutually cavalier attitude that we would have plenty of time to make these things happen.

I spoke to friends and strangers alike of my great love for David and how much we did together when we were growing up, when the truth is that he left the house when I was five or six. I saw him off and on, during holidays and by visiting him at college and medical school, then less and less after I went away to college and never moved back, when I didn't visit our hometown, Houston, more than twice a year. He came to New England only for my college graduation and wedding, which were nearly twelve years apart—just like the span of our ages. So, was I being dishonest?

"Were you close?"

The real answer—or one answer—might be that we weren't *that close* after all, not nearly as close I yearned to be all thirty-five years that we had each other. Another answer might be that David and I were, at least, closer than I was with my brother Tommy, so that always felt like a distinction. But David and Tommy had been thick-as-thieves, bosom-buddies, two-peas-in-a-pod, and any other cliché about closeness for as long as memory served. Only three years apart in age, they had been together in family photos I wasn't born for, attended the same schools, and continued to live together off and on after moving out of our parents' house. They talked almost every day.

David and I will never be as close as I imagined/hoped/expected we could be, and ultimately would be. I thought, like we all think, that we had time.

I had so many fantasies of growing old with him: I thought that one day I would not only buy *him* a lot of beers, but that we would see each other regularly and do more together, and that we would really, deeply get to know each other. That I would listen to more stories of his outdoor adventures and come to understand the thrill, the sense of achievement, the perspective that only summitting a mountain can provide. That he would spend time with my husband and dogs at my house. That I would reveal to him what it meant to make sense of life through words and music. That the gap our age difference had built into our relationship, the thing that had initially made him so much older and farther away, would continue to narrow—in terms of how it felt anyway—as the years passed and we got better at not just being siblings, but also at living, and at connecting with each other.

I expected, at the very least, we'd outlive Mom together. Of all assumptions I could make, that one seemed reasonable.

More than that, I was certain that one day David and I would be not just close—in any and every way it can be described—but *very* close. I wasn't entirely wrong. I just didn't have any idea about how it would happen.

The Dot Stopped

In retrospect, the way David died was completely predictable. In a way, it was even poetic. If I were writing the perfect way for him to go out, it might have been exactly the way it happened. Except for the guesswork and worry.

My musician husband Peyton was on the road in the middle of a national tour but was playing our town on a Thursday in September of 2008. I was thrilled to see him and his bandmates, some of whom I'd been friends with for many years. Wearing a sundress to celebrate the left-over summery heat, I'd happily bounced into the club for soundcheck so I'd get a little extra time with everyone. I helped sling t-shirts at the merch table and danced through every song. The show was joyous. We gave goodbye hugs to the group and headed home for our one night together, high on the concert and the camaraderie.

Twenty minutes past midnight, our phone rang. We wouldn't normally have been up at that time, but we were wide awake that night.

I looked down at the caller ID on the cordless receiver and recognized the number as my mother's. I showed it to Peyton as if I needed him to confirm what I was seeing because it was so odd that anyone, especially she, would be calling at that time. I didn't answer. The ominous feeling of getting a call too late momentarily paralyzed me. We looked at each other for a few seconds, perplexed. She hung up before the call went to voicemail.

Seconds later, it rang again. That time, I answered right away.

"Oh, hi. I'm sorry it's so late," Mom said. "I wasn't sure if I should call or not. I don't know what to think."

"What's going on?" I asked.

"Well," she started, and then hesitated. After a too-long pause, she finally said, "David's missing."

And then jumbled fragments of a story began to spill out: "He was in Colorado with Cheryl and the kids, but they went home yesterday, and he stayed to hike some of the mountains on his own. She called Tommy when she didn't hear from him ... Someone else has the GPS, I don't know ... and, well, it stopped moving. You know, the little dot that shows where he is? It just stopped. I guess it hasn't moved in a while ..." She sounded nervous, but not too nervous. "They've called search and rescue, but it's probably too dark now."

I did a quick calculation counting backward across the time zones, trying to get closer mentally. It would be 10:30 p.m. in Colorado. I sketched a fuzzy picture in my mind from the few details she had told me: my brother's girlfriend Cheryl, her daughter, and our seven-year-old nephew Christopher, Tommy's son, had been camping with him on a trip, but now David was alone. Likely on a mountain. He had a tracking device on him. Disparate members of the family who never spoke to each other directly were discussing things and passing them along like a bad game of telephone. It wasn't clear what the real, full story was. But there was enough concern to warrant a search. The little dot on the GPS, the one that hadn't moved in a while, was my brother.

Mom said she'd call back as soon as she heard something more, and that she was considering flying to Colorado in the morning. Cheryl and David's adventure racing teammate, Shaun, neither of whom she had met in person before, were talking about going too.

She apologized again for calling. Because it was late. But we were up.

Looking Up To

I was born in Houston in 1973 when my mom and dad were thirty-seven and thirty-three and had just been married a couple of years. My two half-brothers, Tommy and David, nine and twelve years older than me respectively, were from my mom's previous marriage. Family lore suggests that when I was born, my big brothers were out being boys digging for crawdads in a ditch near our house. When the news came that I was a girl, their disappointment was palpable. As a form of rebuttal, they took to calling me Bubba, a nickname that is loosely translated, in Texas at least, as "brother."

When I was little, Tommy and David were still living at home with our mom and my dad, so we were a family of five. I was crazy about my big brothers and wanted to be around them all the time. I embraced my nickname wholeheartedly as I emulated their every move.

Because of our age difference, because he taught me lots of things, because he spent so much time entertaining and playing with me, David was often more like a super-fun uncle than a brother. He looked after me, even when he wasn't officially assigned babysitting duty, and learned to love having me for a baby sister.

Family photos visually prove this to me: David, Tommy, and I sit on the golden carpeted stairs—me on David's lap—posing for a Christmas photo with our stockings hung along the banister; David looks down with me as he patiently helps me figure out a jigsaw puzzle; he has his arm slung around my neck as we simultaneously blow out candles on his birthday cake. In a vertical shot, he stands in our verdant backyard wearing his royal blue high school graduation robe and cap, holding me on his hip as naturally as though I were his own kid.

Back then, he devised colorful bedtime stories when he tucked me in at night instead of picking up the nearest children's book. There was an entire series about two characters, Humpy and Bumpy, a camel and a boy with bad acne, who went on adventures together. Every time he came up with a new tale about those guys, we would both laugh so much, it was hard to fall asleep.

David also taught me how to ride my first real bike, a beautiful little red number I got for Christmas when I was five. He helped me go up and down the driveway a million times with the training wheels on and was super patient as I worked myself slowly toward taking them off, building up my confidence as I tried not to wobble. He yelled encouragement when I finally made it to the end of the driveway, and then let go of the seat and I was on my own, flying into the street. When I was stable enough to look back, he was wearing his trademark grin and waving. Nothing pleased me more than making him proud.

When I was two and Tommy and David were eleven and fourteen, my parents built a little get-away in Woodville. Our family drove the two hours to that little East Texas town on every weekend and holiday we could manage, packed tightly into our '70s-style brown-paneled station wagon, me squeezed in the middle of the back seat with my big brothers pressed against me like bookends.

When you're a kid, even small age differences might as well be eternities. The disparity between us was so vast, it seemed my brothers and I had a Grand Canyon of experience between us. I tried my best to earn access to hang out with them but was always "too little." Not only was I the baby, my female status haunted me. Even though I wore t-shirts and sneakers with their old hand-me-down Wranglers, there was no getting around the fact of my gender.

The Big Thicket, the dense, pine-perfumed forest surrounding Woodville, was perfect for adolescent boys. It was a magical-feeling place, full of animals rustling in the dry leaves, with abundant spots to hide in the trees, to hunt the legendary alligator in the lake, to surreptitiously set off fireworks, to raise hell.

Our cabin was set back off a red dirt road, masked by dozens of skinny pines. The walls inside and out were rough-hewn, unpainted wood, and the design was open, with kitchen, living room, and dining room all encompassed in one giant space. The only truly private room, other than the bathroom, was my parents', where I slept on a single bed in a corner. My big brothers got the loft, an enchanted place, an alluring tower, reachable only by a long wooden ladder affixed to the wall of the main room. A ladder that I wasn't even allowed to climb, much less get to the top. It took years before I saw what existed in that private turret.

Up there, two twin mattresses were wedged under the eaves of the roof, intimately close, outfitted with sheets adorned with the names of football teams printed in garish colors. One small window opened out to the forest. I imagined whispers between my brothers at night. Heard roughhousing and laughter. Like a tree-fort built indoors, secret things happened there. I imagined that pacts were made, private handshakes invented. Admission to this boys' clubhouse was rare and coveted.

Ledge-like seats were built under the top railings, on which my brothers perched and yelled down to us on Saturday mornings.

"We want pancakes!" Tommy shouted.

"No, waffles!" David argued.

"We want both!" I yelled, looking up to them, not wanting to pick favorites and not wanting to be left out.

Dad chuckled and put out both the griddle and the waffle iron, in his accommodating way. Before we knew the term, this was how we carb-loaded before we went out for the day.

With a decent-sized, man-made lake just down the road, Tommy and David enthusiastically embraced my father's plan to buy a speedboat so that we could water ski. All of us, including our big red dog Jeff, would jump onboard with a half-dozen towels and a cooler of Cokes, and we would stay out on the lake all afternoon. Daddy had learned to ski back in summer camp when he was my brothers' age, and they picked it up from him naturally, like a second language.

They were always inventing new tricks, trying to outdo each other. I would sit in one of the rear-facing seats in the boat, watching David as he slalomed on one ski, jumping the wake as he crossed it, then leaning hard to the side, kicking up spray. Tommy learned not just how to use skis, but to use his feet, to "barefoot" on the water.

"He's just showing off," my mother would say, exasperated. "I wish he would be more careful."

We stopped at different spots around the horseshoe-shaped body of water to take dips in the lake's officially deemed "swimming areas," bound with wooden barriers built simply with two-by-fours. David taught me how to dive off those railings, empowering me with a skill I felt sure only he and Tommy had ever possessed. I stepped onto one board in the shallow end near the shore and walked it like a balance beam all the way out to the corner, where David was waiting in the deep end.

"Put your arms up and your hands together like this," he said while pointing the tips of his fingers skyward in an inverted V.

"Is it deep?" I asked.

"Just deep enough. You don't ever want to dive if it's shallow."

"I can't see the bottom." The lake suffered aesthetically from the native dirt and was a murky, opaque brown, but I was eager to prove myself.

"Trust me, young'un," he said. "I've got you."

I took the leap of faith, and David grabbed me the minute I emerged from under water like a fishing bobber. He held me in his arms and laughed. "You got it! Just like a pro," he said, always ready to give me a boost. At moments like those, I glowed with a sense of accomplishment, my brother helping me feel less like a baby, a bit more like a big kid, like him.

After kindergarten, I got my own small pair of wooden skis. This was a monumental rite of passage, as it provided the opportunity to join the ranks. Together, my brothers showed me how to "get up"—the way to let the boat yank you out of the dark water and up onto the surface of the lake. ("Staying up" was another thing.) They yelled to me from the back of the boat, over the noise of the outboard motor.

"Keep your arms straight!" Tommy hollered. "Don't pull up!"

"Keep your tips out of the water!" David yelled.

As Dad pushed the throttle forward, they continued to shout their support: "You're doing it, Bubba!" I trusted them even when that felt completely unnatural, and the next thing I knew, I was plucked from the water and gliding over the surface at what felt like warp speed, probably only about twenty miles an hour.

Though I'll never understand how, David and Tommy even convinced our parents to get them dirt bikes to ride up at the cabin. They had cool helmets and special racing shirts made of dense material, which I imagine was supposed to offer protection if you fell off. They would jump on those bikes and peel out of the gravel driveway, yelling all the way. They revved through the fiery red roads, disappearing in orange clouds of dust. I never knew where they went, and I always felt left behind.

Years later, I found one of those motorcycling shirts abandoned in a closet after my brothers had gone to college. It was dingy yellow and dirt-stained with green rubbery lettering—about the unsexiest article of clothing you'd think a girl coming of age in the '80s might want—but I adored it and wore the hell out of it, much to my mother's chagrin.

The face of the cabin, which had a wide unrailed porch along the length of it, was not square with the road; it was positioned at a pretty angle, like a model striking a pose. My mom and dad were both so enamored with the trees that they had adjusted the builder's designs to ensure no more than necessary were cut down to accommodate the structure; a notch had even been carved out of the middle of the porch floor to accommodate the trunk of a fat pine.

Beneath the porch, snakes slithered into the shade, enjoying respite from the heat. We always knew they were down there, and we generally coexisted just fine, though early on, David shared some wilderness education with me.

"Hey, darlin'," he said, pulling me up onto his lap on one of the benches on the porch. "There are two kinds of snakes that are both really pretty and look almost exactly the same, except one of them is nice and the other one is poisonous."

"Really?"

"Mmm hmm," he said calmly. "And it's important to know the difference. They both have red, black, and yellow stripes, but in different orders. There's a little rhyme to help you remember. It goes 'Red and black, friend of Jack, red and yellow, kill a fellow.'"

That was like poetry to me with its simple rhyme scheme, and I recited it to myself a lot. One morning on a later trip, awake before everyone else as usual, I walked out onto the porch and saw a brightly colored snake moving through the brown pine needles on the ground below. So, I started reciting the words, initially sing-song and innocent, while I took a closer look. Just minutes after my yell, David had swiftly chopped up the coral snake into tiny wriggling pieces with a hoe. He might as well have slayed a dragon.

That was one of those mornings I could have been minding myself quietly indoors while the family slept in. I was an early riser and often took to drawing before the rest of the cabin awoke. I had a bunch of art supplies in the top of a red-painted chest—crayons, scissors, markers, paper, and glue—and pulled them out each time we were there in order to create a new set of paper rabbits. This series was like paper dolls, except I hated dolls and I loved animals, so I decided to create and dress up an array of bunnies. Two inches high, these teeny figures got outfitted in clothes with itty bitty tabs to hold them over the rabbits' shoulders and onto their hips. In the spirit of the place,

I made sure they had practical clothes like t-shirts, shorts, and bathing suits, and little Wrangler jeans.

I listened and watched, mimicked and revered. There is nothing quite like a big brother, never mind two. Even as Bubba, it took a while to realize I just wasn't going to grow up to be a boy. I would never be their brother.

Appeals

When I got the call that David was missing, I didn't even know he was on a trip, but he often was, and he certainly didn't give me the heads-up every time, or even most times. I knew that every moment he could manage to get away from his day job as a radiologist, he traveled all over the world for any number of endurance sports and outdoor excursions—and for pure pleasure: scuba diving in Mexico, triathlons in Greenland, mountain biking through the jungles of Costa Rica, bone fishing in the Christmas Islands, cyclocross racing in Rhode Island, bungee jumping in Australia, ultramarathon running across Colorado. His entire adult life had been spent seeking out the next thrilling journey and the next big physical achievement in a beautiful, wild place.

Earlier that summer, David and his team of four had competed in one of the most difficult, internationally acclaimed adventure races—Primal Quest—which took place that year in Big Sky, Montana. After trail runs, biking, kayaking, snowshoeing, and rappelling through five hundred miles of rugged terrain, they came in fifth place worldwide. I still beam with pride when I look at a glossy color photo in which they are all triumphantly holding up the American flag in front of them like a bright, patriotic shield.

When I hung up the phone after speaking with my mom, my brain hadn't fully accepted or even deciphered exactly what I'd heard. I just recapped the facts like a journalist for Peyton, who was standing by looking anxious. David had stayed in Colorado to climb mountains by himself. Later, I would learn these were part of a large mountain range called Blanca Massif, home to a number of Colorado's famous fourteeners, fifty-four peaks statewide that stand over fourteen thousand feet in altitude. Apparently, his newest athletic quest was to bag them all. No one knew where he was.

Mom had reported that Tommy was putting on a brave face: "David probably has two broken legs," he told her. "He must be stuck somewhere eating a Power Bar and laughing about it."

Peyton poured me a whiskey and pressed the cold glass into my hand. We stared at each other some more, wide-eyed, not knowing what to say. Our two dogs paced around us, unsure about the energy that had just entered the room, searching our faces for clues. It was late, and I was suddenly way too awake.

Was David lost? It seemed impossible, given his extensive experience with orienteering. Was he freezing cold? Those mountains had snow even in the summer. Was he scared? Doubtful. I couldn't think of a time he had been stressed out or nervous, ever. Not even when he had rounds in the emergency room doing his medical residency. This was sort of reassuring, the way he had always been reassuring.

Peyton and I had a brief conversation about the possibility of two broken legs. It became more like bargaining. And maybe a little bit like praying. *Alright, Universe, if it can just be two broken legs, maybe he'll get the message and stop all this craziness. If he's only injured and stuck somewhere, everything will be okay.* Deep down, both of us knew David well enough to know that nothing would keep him from tackling big challenges outdoors. Other than the possibility we refused to talk about.

I finally went to bed, not entirely sleeping, but dozing occasionally while clutching the phone to my chest. It rang around dawn.

"Nothing yet," Mom said. "It was too dark last night. They'll try again when the sun comes up." In the meantime, she had booked a flight to Colorado Springs, the closest airport to Alamosa, where David's RV was parked in an open area below the mountain range. She would meet Cheryl and Shaun there.

I nodded off for a while, my dog pressed against my side protectively, as she always knew when something was wrong. A couple of hours later, when the phone rang again, still held tight in my fist, it took three rings before I could muster the courage to pick up.

Dr. Dave

When I was ten years old, David was in medical school in Galveston after finishing his pre-med degree at the University of Texas at Austin. As part of his MD education, he got his very own human cadaver to study. Listening to stories about learning anatomy on a real body enthralled me, and I was thrilled when Mom and I went to visit him one weekend so I would have a chance to see it.

David's dissection class took place in a sterile-feeling white room, colossal in my memory, with the highest ceilings I'd ever seen. Upon entry, we were greeted by pristine shelves holding row upon row of glass jars with various body parts submerged in fluid. These included items of great fascination, such as a series of hands with the skin peeled back to show the veins and tendons and an entire head with the top of the skull removed in a neat circle to view the brain. Full skeletons were on display in two corners of the room. Plastic models of muscle systems perched on tables. Trays covered in white paper held carefully arranged stainless steel instruments. To me, the whole place was a museum of scientific wonder.

Just past these curiosities were the cadavers. Long silver boxes with two doors on top that opened like small wardrobes were set on wheeled metal tables, lined up in an orderly way down both sides of the classroom. When David showed us his table and I carefully peered inside the box, I had no idea what to expect. His cadaver was female, and one of her breasts was gone, cut away like chicken meat from her body. She smelled funny, but not too bad.

This woman's body, donated to help further science, was the coolest thing I'd ever seen. I was proud of my fearlessness, which I might not have considered had Mom not been standing in the corner of the room avoiding the box, looking pale and sweaty. Having seen a dead body gave me bragging rights in the school-yard, and years later, I would still remember it and tell Peyton I wanted to donate my body to a medical school, inspired by that experience.

We all liked having a doctor in the family. Not only was it a source of general pride, it was practical. One of us often called David with a simple question about odd symptoms or to ask for a recommendation of treatment for a friend's malady. Occasionally, I took advantage of having him write me an off-the-record prescription. Sometimes, it was simply easier and more pleasant to have David treat us than anyone else. When we were nervous, he was calm; he had the skills and the tools. Plus, he knew us and loved us.

During a summer when I was in Houston between college semesters, I sliced through my thumb using a paper cutter, and getting stitches at the emergency room with a gruff physician had freaked me out. Instead of going back to him to have my sutures removed, David came by the record store where I worked. He pulled alcohol swabs, tweezers, and scissors from his pocket, with which he made quick work of cleaning up my healing finger. Why go back to the doctor's office to get a little thread removed when my sweet big brother could take care of this chore between the Pop and Latin sections?

Years before, after a legendary night of drinking, testosterone got the best of Tommy and he decided he could smash a glass on his head at a bar. Instead of going to the hospital, Tommy went to our brother. At their med school fraternity house, David and his medical school buddies surrounded him like he was a lab rat, eager to practice. They sewed up his bloody head, and Tommy was relieved to have his brother take care of him too. Win, win.

Mom had also benefitted from his knowledge. After a bad cat scratch, she developed bright red lines threading up her arms. A quick call to Dr. Dave assured her that she needed antibiotics STAT for blood poisoning.

In my early twenties, I battled traffic for an hour to reach Northwest Houston Radiology where I proudly announced to the receptionist at the desk, "I'm here to see Dr. David Boyd."

"I'll let him know you're here," she said brightly. I sat in the sunny waiting room for a few minutes, and then saw him striding confidently down the hall in his cornflower blue scrubs and running sneakers.

"Hey, darlin'," he said with his soft Texan lilt as he gave me a powerful hug and a peck.

David escorted me down a fluorescently bright hallway to the office he shared with the other doctors in his group. As we entered, my eyes adjusted to the darkness, and it reminded me of the back room of the reptile house at the zoo where the vampire bats are housed. As kids, we used to gather around their faintly lit habitats, noses pressed against the glass, staring intently at their stretchy winged shrouds, peering into their upside-down faces, pointing to the black pools of real blood set out for them.

In this cave, the only light emanated from computer screens and a few light boxes hung on the walls. Radiologists hunched over eerie black and white illuminated images scrutinizing even more closely than we used to stare at those bats. The X-rays and MRI scans, mammograms and ultrasounds, showing the soft interiors of other people's bodies, looked like confusing blurs or abstract art to me. There was nothing clear like a broken arm bone. These experts, however, inspected the minutiae for errant specks or dangerously enlarged areas no one else could see.

I wasn't just there for a tour of his workplace. I had been having chronic headaches. It was concerning to our mother most of all, so she asked David to perform a CAT scan on me. We treated it more like a game, an opportunity to hang out and test the equipment, than anything serious. But I inherited her worrier genes, so part of me was a little edgy. Still, there was no one on Earth more comforting than David, always self-assured and generously reassuring to others. If there was something wrong, I'd rather he told me than anyone else.

The fact that I could have a relatively complex diagnostic test with him instead of a random stranger mostly made me feel special rather than concerned. He had always been a scientist, conducting experiments since we were kids, wanting to learn from the results. I was pleased to be his guinea pig any day.

In a room labeled *Computerized Axial Tomography*, he and his associate didn't even have me change into a johnny. I just had to remove my earrings.

"It's only your head we're examining," he said with a chuckle.

"Ha, ha," I said as I positioned myself on the long narrow bed of the machine. He retreated behind a pane of glass as my head slid into the donut hole in the enormous machine. He told me to be as still as possible as whirring sounds started up, swirling around my head.

David continued to chat with me breezily by microphone while I stared into the dark, and I thought back to the head in the jar in his medical school. When the procedure was over, my brother let me into the cubicle to look at the computer screen with him. It was bizarre to see the slices of my head looking like misshapen, unappetizing pieces of bread.

The conclusion?

"Textbook normal," he happily pronounced, then without missing a beat, turned to me and said, "Lunch?"

Found

"I'm at the airport now. Anne. It's not good."

Mom paused for a long time before she said the rest: "They found his body."

This didn't compute. This wasn't a possibility. This made no sense. It was so far beyond "not good."

"He fell."

She wasn't crying. How was she not crying?

I was barely able to respond. "Oh, Mom."

I stayed on the phone with her as she checked in at the ticket counter, while she sat in the waiting area at the gate until her flight boarded, during the time she handed her ticket to the airline's agent, while she somehow managed to put one foot in front of the other and walk down the long ramp to the plane, as she searched for and located her seat assignment while the intercom squawked loudly in the background. We weren't having a real conversation; it was as though I was holding her hand, virtually. I was mostly listening to her going through these impossible motions, occasionally saying something non-committal like "uh huh" or "okay" or "I love you" just so she knew I was still there on the end of the line.

She didn't want to hang up, but it's all I wanted to do. I felt horrible for her, but my brain was swirling, and I didn't feel present either in the airport with her or in my own house, where I paced from room to room. I couldn't breathe properly; I couldn't process what she had just told me; I didn't know how to make words; I had no idea what to say to her. Finally, the flight attendants announced that electronic devices were no longer permitted, as the plane was preparing to take off. She promised to call when she got there.

The moment I hung up, I found myself falling onto the downstairs bathroom floor, howling, holding onto myself with both arms, rocking on the cold ceramic tiles. I wanted to be put inside something smaller. I needed to be boxed in; I was going to break apart. I scared the dogs, but they pressed against me with all their weight, as if they knew what to do. Peyton ran down the stairs looking at me wild-eyed with fear, with helplessness, with knowing, with not knowing what to do. He and the dogs all held their bodies against me. I sensed I was on the verge of detonating. I didn't know if my center would hold. Parts of me wanted to rip apart like shrapnel, like cracked glass, like rubble and rocks. I thought I might—I would—soon become a horrible disaster area.

After my initial near-explosion, I was surprised that being inside was no comfort. The closeness of walls did not provide a hug of support as it might in other situations. Rather, by being indoors, a stifled sense consumed me. I was squeezed in, suffocating. I felt jailed by the words I heard. The framework of the house caved in on me; incomprehensible reality shuttered me. All I could think was, *Get me out of here.*

It was a sudden impulse, as sure as any I've ever had, to climb. I told Peyton we had to go, now. He was surprised, but game.

I hiked through my mind while simultaneously our bodies moved up and onto Mount Nonotuck, the tall and sturdy mountain behind our house. We had a secret—think unauthor- ized—access point at the end of the street where electrical poles marched straight up in a soldierly way and a thin line was tram- pled in the grass on the left-hand side toward the access path.

I couldn't help but think of David's ascent. *Am I attempting some parallel path? Does matching his footfall, however far away, help to make sense of this impossibility?*

As if by scaling rocks, moving through trees, putting myself in a place where I had a similar vantage point as he had last, I might gain some clarity. As if I might feel what he was feeling as my legs burned, my lungs heaved. As if by going outward and upward, I could right his fall, pull the accident backward through time, a film reel played in reverse, spliced, played again forward, differently. As if by going upward, toward the sky, I might reach him in time.

Familiar mosses graced the shady spots with green. The long, smooth body of a fallen tree that we always stepped over, the dogs jumped over, as usual. We had joked in the past, calling this verdant stretch *Fern Gully* like the Disney film, its abundant ferns prettily bordering the stretch where heavy rainfall carved a gouge. It felt safe there—protected, yet open. And so very alive.

We climbed past the telltale scratches of black bears on a pine, chunks of bark gathering at the base of the trunk. Stepped over rocky ledge-like steps, danced around roots and stumps. The strain of the physical work of moving against gravity felt essential: the push and pull of my knees, the labor of my breath, the blood pulsing in my ears, drowning out the internal chant: *He is dead, he is dead, he is dead.* Upward, always upward, toward the sky to breathe, as if coming from some ocean depth back to the surface.

We had done this hike how many times? That day it was different and also, reassuringly, the same. The dogs raced ahead, and we met them where a slim railing underlined the horizon emphatically, where the expansive Connecticut River Valley spread below us, majestic as the many paintings it has inspired.

When I saw the chunks of gravel underfoot, I thought of the scree that must have made him slip. What did the shards look like, feel like, sound like clicking underfoot where he stood? I thought of just how far down, how many feet this must be, from the top of the mountain to the town below. I thought about falling. And yet, I climbed.

I imagined David's final lookout.

How had I not sensed it? We found out later that David had died two days before he was found. Somehow, during that time, I continued to laugh, sing, breathe. Naïve, innocently unaware. I should have sensed a seismic shift, even all the way from Colorado to Massachusetts.

What if no one had ever told me? What if I didn't know now? David could still be out there somewhere grinning, feet wide apart, arms open, on a mountaintop, hugging the sky. I might run into him. I might find him.

His Hands

David's hands were tremendous tools. No mere devices to hold a pen or throw a ball. These hands were practiced, disciplined, fine-tuned.

Medical school had taught him how to thread catheters and send teensy cameras through arteries, set bones, delicately cut flesh, stitch like a gifted seamstress. They held X-rays up toward the light to translate a visual language.

His hands were always tan and rugged from the outdoors, scarred from a lifetime's adventures. They steered him on special bicycle grips and gripped the horns on horse saddles. They pulled him up cliff walls and belayed him into canyons. They grabbed other hands to pull people up. He latched ski buckles, tied boot laces, fitted snowshoes. Those fingers learned elaborate knots, how to quickly make camp, to use navigational tools. His palm was a level surface for a compass.

His hands tinkered with dozens of mountain bikes, not just repairing them, but also enhancing them, creating new devices, tricking them out: a map holder, a snack container, a retractable dog leash for pulling his teammates up hills. David's hands held onto the handlebars of my first little bike, keeping me steady when he taught me to ride.

In high school, David's hands used to make questionable science experiments, punch Tommy, hang onto the rope as he water-skied. His hands packed away sleeping bags, bike shorts, maps, and rifles. They drove trucks, boats, RVs, dirt bikes, a motorcycle. They pulled the ripcord on his parachute, confidently let go when bungee jumping. They clasped paddles, cast fishing lines, adjusted goggles and scuba breathing apparatuses.

They tended to blistered feet on the trail. They handed his race prizes to others. Their warmth transferred comfort, encouragement.

They wore gloves, but never a ring.

Those hands held the hands of so many pretty girls, squeezed Gran's hand as she got older and older, hung onto mine during her funeral. Carried our niece and nephew up onto his shoulders, up into the air. They threw duck decoys for his beloved black lab Harley, and held his cat, Sam, aloft for kisses.

Finally, David's hands lost their grip one afternoon in Colorado, finding no purchase on the loose scree. His eyes were blind with wind or snow and his hands couldn't find a ledge. They reached out and grabbed nothing but air. He extended those hands that had helped so many, and no one was there with a hand for him.

Hangover

When something seemingly impossible happens, it's hard to know how to move at all. In the immediate aftermath of David's death, I moved in impulsive, twitchy ways.

Peyton had been on tour playing guitar in his friends' band, Silver Jews, for a couple of weeks before the accident—calling me each night from Indianapolis, Detroit, Pontiac, Toronto— but fate somehow brought him home to play in Northampton that night. Because Peyton was with me when I got the call, I've always felt the universe threw me a bone that day.

But he was scheduled to leave town again because the band had a gig the following night. It was an easy decision to go to Boston with him; as much as I was well-practiced at holding down the fort in his absence, I couldn't imagine being left alone then. And I didn't even want to be at home. Getting away from where I heard the worst news I'd ever received felt necessary and urgent.

Even though I drive us almost all the time, Peyton wisely took the wheel that day. He gave me two peach-colored tablets of Valium and strapped me into the passenger seat. Moving down Interstate 91, I stared ahead at the same road I had seen hundreds of times before, the same turns and signs, dumbly wondering how the world continued to exist, just as it was, just as it always had been. Yellow paint continued to stitch a broken line down the middle of the asphalt. Trees, energetically green, still reached toward the sky. A sense of numbness and resignation set in as I slumped in my seat. Peyton offered to take me home and bail out on the show any time, but I kept insisting that I needed him to play, I needed to hear the band, that he shouldn't miss a gig, that the show—like the world—should go on.

In the cool darkness of the basement club, his bandmates, who had seen me so jovial at the show just the night before—when I was dancing in the crowd, helping set up the merch table, flitting around like some grand hostess—put their arms around me and let me cry all over them. I was plied with beers, buoyed by the raucous energy of the opening band, and soothed by the familiar melodies of the headliners.

The next night, I decided to go on with them to the Music Hall of Williamsburg in Brooklyn. I wanted more of the band, more of Peyton, and more of the escape from reality that being on tour provides.

While we were packing the car, Tommy called to inform me—rather than discuss with me—that David's memorial would be held at his stepmother's church in Houston. Juggling luggage and guitars while holding the cell phone to my ear, I said I thought a park would make a lot more sense for David, since he wasn't religious, and if he had a church, it was The Great Outdoors.

In a tone I had found condescending my whole life, Tommy said, "Anne, we don't have time to do something like that, *in a park*," as if I had asked to bring everyone together on the moon. "Let's just get it done."

"Why would we want to just 'get it done'?" I flamed. "This is *David* we're talking about. It should be special. He was special. He didn't even like church."

"Who's going to plan that? You? You're not even here." Tommy reminded me that I was the one who had moved away, and it stung.

Standing in the middle of the street, I yelled, "Well David didn't have an extraordinary life so that we could have a generic, boring church service for him!"

Tommy and I had never been what anyone would exactly call close, never quite understood each other or each other's life choices. I was an artist with tattoos, living in Massachusetts; liberal, mission-driven, and sometimes introverted; volunteering in an animal rescue; and working in non-profit marketing communications instead of at some job that paid a lot. Tommy sold mortgages; loved to wheel and deal; voted Republican and played golf; and acted as though making money was not only the best goal in life, but the only one. The most significant thing we had in common—by far—was our mutual love of David. We were equally feverish with grief. I was furious with the way he continued to treat me like a baby even at thirty-five years old. I was furious that he insisted on putting me in my place. I was furious about my helplessness. I was furious about everything. I hung up on him.

It's absurd that the bereaved should have to begin making plans for a big event the moment after they are notified of a death. It seems to me that funeral arrangements should be put off for a while, until the living have stopped reeling and can begin to think clearly at all. We no longer have to bury a body right away because it might decompose in front of us. With a shock like David gave us, we couldn't have been any more ill-equipped to handle logistics.

Once in Brooklyn, Peyton and I waited outside in our car for the rest of the band to arrive for sound check. It started to rain.

Mom called from Colorado, and Peyton sat patiently in the driver's seat while I talked to her. She told me about arriving at the airport in Colorado Springs and finding Shaun and Cheryl camped out in the facility's chapel. Drops beat against the windshield loudly, and I strained to hear her. As I pressed my cell phone to my ear, she described their drive down to Alamosa, a small town close to the mountain range, and the incredible mass of people who had showed up to search for my brother.

Leslie, another teammate, would later tell me about how she immediately jumped in her car upon hearing that David was lost and drove a thousand miles without stopping in order to be there. When I expressed my surprise at her and the rest of David's teammates' unflinching action, she said matter-of-factly, "That's just what you do. It's 'man down.'"

During the call, Mom recapped what she had learned and what followed: search and rescue had retrieved my brother's body from a spot high up on a mountain called Little Bear, apparently his third peak to climb in one day. Leslie arrived just in time for the stretcher to be brought down, and immediately puked at the base of the mountain. Mom, Shaun, and Cheryl then traveled together to the coroner's office in Colorado Springs. The staff there apparently tried to prepare everyone by saying, "He doesn't look good." I asked her what that meant. You know, other than dead.

David always looked good. He usually looked downright gorgeous. My girlfriends all had crushes on him. He was classically tall, dark, and handsome, plus he had that sculpted body he trained so hard for, sweet hazel-green eyes, and a grin that broke hearts. Even after a ten-day race with no showering, he just looked tough and rugged. Even when he shaved his legs to reduce drag and bike faster, he was manly. Even when he buzzed all his dark hair because it was more comfortable under a bike helmet, it gave him a soldierly allure.

In my mind's eye, being in the coroner's office was like a scene on *Law & Order* in which a traumatized family member has to identify a murder victim. I could only picture a TV drama version in my head because what Mom had to do—confirm that the body was that of her son—was nearly impossible to believe. I imagine they drew a curtain, and David's now-cold body was positioned behind a large pane of glass under a sanitized white sheet on a gurney against a wall of institutional sea green tile, as if keeping things clean and hospital-like would somehow anesthetize the situation.

I was two thousand miles away during the identification. I listened hard to the surreal scene, wanting the details regardless of how painful they were to hear. I had questions. There were things I needed to know. Things no one should ever have to ask or know. Mom said he was bloody. This shocked me. Because hadn't he fallen—and broken somehow?

"What happened? What did they say?" The underlying question was "What actually killed him?" but I couldn't quite manage to phrase it that way yet. It seemed a stupid question after a two-hundred-foot fall, but surely there were specifics. There were.

"A rib snapped and pierced his heart," Mom told me. "It was instantaneous, they said." Except for the falling part, I thought. Did it feel like a second? Or like forever? Was it like slow motion? Or was it so fast, he didn't even have time to realize what was happening?

My brother broke on the inside. So, what was bloody? I considered the blood we share. I remember saying, somewhat irrelevantly, "David will always be a part of me." Somehow, it felt gory in a new way that the blood was outside, conspicuous. I had thought he would be intact at least, as if this mattered. I wondered if he was naked or dressed in his hiking clothes and whether they had used the sheet technique. This I didn't ask.

Mom was impressed with the helmet he had been wearing. "Those really work!" she said.

"What do you mean?" Nothing had worked.

"Well, his head was perfect."

Forty-seven years before, David emerged, separating from our mother's body. I think of how she must have held him, a soft, tiny new form, everything ahead of him. I can't quite reconcile how she had to see him again, that last time, grown so strong, independent, successful, adored—and so very dead. If I had been in her place, I would have wanted to hold him again. I would have insisted. His big, experienced, muscular body, defined by motion, now so still. More still than "still" can define.

Peyton and I hunkered down in the car as the rain drummed against the roof harder and harder, blurring our view through the windshield. Everything was blurry.

That night, as Peyton's band played their satisfying blend of psychedelic country, I stood in the balcony of the music hall with a couple of our best friends from college, who lived in the city. They had been brought in for relief, for support.

I don't know how many Cosmos I drank, but the vodka was doing its job. I remember sobbing when the band broke into

"Pretty Eyes," one of my favorites, equal parts eviscerating and consoling right then:

Some people think the stars are the headlights of angels,
driving from Heaven to save us, to save us.
Look in the sky—
They're driving from Heaven into our eyes.

I cried and cried and cried some more, drenching my shirt and swaying in that back corner of the balcony with the sense that I might never be able to stop. I begged those angels to save me.

The next morning, I woke up in our friend Andrew's apartment. Once I oriented myself, I realized I had to throw up. Urgently. Andrew's roommate was in the bathroom; the shower was running. Andrew was asleep on the couch. Desperate, I crawled out his bedroom window onto a little side roof and got rid of what was left of the poison I had drunk.

After the rain the night before, the day was clear and incongruously beautiful. I went on to the Bowery Ballroom in Manhattan for another Silver Jews show. "I just feel better when I'm hearing music," I said to Peyton. When the songs ended, my mind went back to the grim reality. That night we bunked up with another friend, and in the stairwell of his apartment building, I paused and looked down the many, many flights and asked no one in particular, "How many feet do you think that is? Do you think it's as many as two hundred?"

Peyton had to go on to the next town with the band and I had to go home eventually, so I retrieved my car from outside Andrew's apartment and drove the three hours north to our house. When

I walked in, our kitchen was covered with cutout paper hearts. All sizes and colors were pasted to the cabinets, the windows, the refrigerator, the counter tops, as if a kindergarten classroom had brought their construction paper and scissors and gone wild. These symbols of love overwhelmed me with their multitude. A giant bouquet of flowers was poised on the counter. Cards were on display. It was impossible not to smile in awe of this gift. Kim, my dear friend and workmate, had broken into my house to remind me how loved I was.

While I had been away, David's memorial had been scheduled for later that week. In the meantime, I went back to work. I met with my two staff members. They gave me a lovely calendar with X-ray pictures of flowers because they knew David had been a radiologist. I told them how much I loved it, what a blessing it had been to spend time with Peyton and the band, and what a gift it was to have had a brother like mine. They looked a little anxious about me, sitting in the chairs on the opposite side of my desk. I was too cheerful. Too full of gratitude. They knew me.

After our meeting, I ran to the bathroom and threw up again.

Feast for the Eyes

After returning from New York, I felt a deep longing I could most closely relate to hunger; I was suddenly starved for my brother's face. I had pictures of David printed at home: several from our wedding, a few from growing up and from holiday visits to Houston, but it wasn't enough. After combing through my digital photos, though thrilled with each discovery, I was still unsatisfied. Though I knew I'd soon have access to my mother's epic collection of pictures neatly organized by year in their original paper envelopes from the sixties and seventies, I was impatient for more.

If I could stuff myself with images of my brother, emblazoning him in my mind over and over, would I find some solace? By seeing him in quantity, would I reassure myself that he had really existed? Did I think if I studied his face that I could somehow summon him? And how many pictures would be enough? What was missing?

Something came to me: when we had talked earlier that summer, David mentioned his excitement at having secured a photographer to join his team at his upcoming adventure race. For the first time, they would have pictures taken while they competed. It meant that, for once, an entire expedition experience would be documented and no one on MOAT would have to think about taking a single shot.

MOAT stood for "Mother of all Teams." I'm pretty sure David came up with that name, and I'm pretty sure I didn't find it terribly clever. In fact, I remember thinking it was silly. Aspirational, sure, but not terribly creative. But it was just a label, one that worked and one that made him and the rest of the crew happy.

"Adventure racing" seemed a term coined just for him, marrying his love of exploration and physical competition. These events are designed like extended—and far more complex—triathlons in the wilderness. Endurance is tested during long stretches of alternating disciplines. Core elements usually include trail running, mountain biking, and paddling kayaks or canoes. Sometimes, the contests add swimming, climbing, horseback riding, snowshoeing, whitewater rafting, canyoneering, or some trendy athletic activity like altitude running to the mix.

This all must be accomplished successfully in a co-ed team with two to four other athletes working harmoniously while simultaneously determining the fastest route using maps and orienteering skills. Courses are rugged and unmarked. Gear, food, and water have to be carried. Checkpoints must be met. Also called "expedition racing," these trials often take place for several days, covering hundreds of miles, and have unsubtle names like Grizzly Man, Eco-Challenge, and the aforementioned Primal Quest. Just finishing is often considered a victory. In 2005, three years before his death, David, Leslie, and Shaun had won the National Championships.

I didn't have any photographs of David doing the thing he loved most, the kind of thing that, arguably, also cost him his life. A quick online search reminded me of the photographer's name. I located an email address and sent a quick message: *Hi Glennon, I'm the famous Dave Boyd's little sister. He was so psyched to have you on board at Primal Quest. I'm grateful for any images of him I can get. In that vein, can I trouble you to get a disc of those shots at some point? I'm happy to pay you for anything.*

He wrote back, short and sweet: *Yes, I will send you a CD or DVD for free. He was a friend, and that's the least I can do.*

In the meantime, he sent a link to a blog post where he had put together a short photo journal of the race. In the section Day 1, I found a group shot of the four MOAT contenders mid-stride on a rocky path, each donning helmets, packs, sunglasses, and royal blue bibs with the number thirty-five printed boldly in white on their chests. Determined expressions worn on all their faces, David has the tip of his tongue clenched in his lips and a small bloody scrape already on his shin. Next, a shot looking up toward the team on a snowy slope as they raise their fists in the air, David grinning broadly, as if already victorious. Further photos show the team on bikes, hiking poles sticking out of packs and headlamps attached to helmets, with my brother leading them in a straight line, a method I would learn later was a technique for strategically reducing drag.

Glenn's text included juicy details to accompany the pictures: my brother and his teammate Nathan "Wink" capsized while paddling a swollen river with Class 4 Rapids, and, he explained, David had dangerously poor buoyancy after having "burped" most of the air out of his dry suit beforehand for the sake of comfort. Despite what anyone might presume about the female members on these co-ed teams, Leslie "was ALWAYS the first member of Team MOAT ready to go," he wrote alongside a photo of her studying maps. And, shown through an array of pale soles, he demonstrated that even on the course, my brother was always Dr. Dave, taking care of everyone's blistered, aching feet.

In one of my favorites, Leslie and David smile at each other knowingly, delightedly, as Wink and Shaun smile straight into the camera, a broad expanse of purple mountains behind them as dusk descends. In the final photo, Glenn captured the team in bright sunshine after finishing 512 miles in eight days: as they pedal toward the ribbon at the finish line, Wink raises his hands off his handlebars, Shaun and Leslie high five each other, and my brother calmly brings up the rear.

Perhaps dearest to me in the entire series, though, is an image not of anyone racing; it's a sideline shot of David eating cereal. Shirtless and standing, he cradles a bowl with his left hand and holds a plastic spoon with the right. Even technically resting, he looks ahead, not at what he's eating, sunglasses on his head, tendon bulging in his forearm, all of him ready to spring.

Later that year, I discovered that Primal Quest had created documentary videos of each of their competitions and eagerly awaited my ordered copy in the mail. Like a voracious animal, I stared at the TV screen expecting to devour a picture of my brother *in motion*—surely, the only non-professional team to make the top five finishers would be there—but MOAT had either not been filmed or had ended up on the cutting room floor.

A friend of David's excitedly mentioned the DVD on Facebook sometime later, and I couldn't help thinking he was searching for the same kind of reminder, the same consolation. *Don't bother*, I posted. *He isn't in there.*

Thank heavens, Glenn was.

Figure Drawing

When Shaun told me about the adventure races, he explained how they would camp—ever so briefly—wherever they could, regardless of weather or locale, strategically stopping around 4:30 in the morning to grab just an hour or so of sleep. If it was scheduled this way, right before dawn, he said, you could trick your body into thinking it had a full night's rest by the increasing sunlight. It sounded equal parts romantic and torturous.

I used to imagine David sleeping outside in the wilderness, under a ceiling of stars. I could almost hear the crickets rubbing their legs together, playing a lullaby to him, or the water of a nearby river rushing by like soothing white noise. I saw him snug in a goose-down sleeping bag, reflecting on the day's journey—considering whether they had been fast enough, if he'd provided the best guidance for his team, analyzing the choices he had made. He was likely planning mentally for the day ahead, the course laid out in his mind. Whether facing mountains or desert, rocks or snow, intense heat or a shrill wind, he would be ready. Body kick-started, they would hit the trail again at sunrise.

David's days of working in the ER during his medical residency had been good training: working under pressure for long stretches, not sweating the small stuff, making definitive decisions, and sleeping on cue. He could sleep *anywhere*. Back then, it was often in a doctors' break room on a cot under fluorescent lights or in his Jeep in the parking lot, with the seat tilted back. It was a specialized skill, this instant nap—arms crossed over his chest, hands tucked into his armpits, head back, ankles overlapped. Within seconds of lying down, he'd be out. Then just a little shut-eye, and he was ready to go again.

He'd never had to condition himself for running hard and recharging quickly; even as a kid, he'd run himself ragged and then crash out. Falling asleep seemed an in-borne trait; I'd witnessed this natural ability as far back as those days at the cabin in East Texas. After a long day of skiing and swimming, David would shower, lie down on the couch, and start breathing heavily right away. Then he'd be up and ready for dinner in minutes.

Once David was part of a radiological practice, he would schedule himself to be on call for weeks straight with no days off to earn extended time to journey somewhere exciting. In addition to earning extensive vacation time after brutal stretches of work, his job provided a generous paycheck for airfare, equipment, and even an RV for the team. It helped them travel to exotic locales like Moab, the Florida swamplands, the Badlands of South Dakota. With bunk beds built in, they could sleep all over the country.

I remember so well what he looked like asleep. His slumbering face always appeared peaceful and calm—so content, there was often a trace of a smile on his face.

Now I try to imagine him dead as if sleeping, since I have no other reference. Other than that cadaver back in his medical school classroom, that body which was so clinical, it belied ever having lived. I recreate David's carved-looking cheekbones, the laughter lines around his eyes, that crescent scar on his chin— picked up during some outing—and those long, wild eyebrows that we joked needed grooming. His eyes are closed, but he is no longer just sleeping.

Once David told me about learning that a racing friend had been treed by a grizzly bear while hiking. Up in the branches, she was stuck, and no one was around to save her. "What happened?" I asked of this misadventure, assuming an impressive rescue story lay ahead.

"She got eaten," he said, matter-of-factly. He took it in stride, while I was horrified. He told me frankly that if this was the way he went out, so be it.

"At least he was doing what he loved."

Friends, strangers, and I repeated that line countless times in the aftermath of David's death. Unlike so many platitudes, this statement provided comfort. There is something to be said for dying when you are happiest, most satisfied, at the top of your game. No one who knew him would have wanted David to suffer a long illness, to have a meaningless accident like a car crash, or probably even to have been incapacitated by the natural course of old age. If he'd had to choose, I think he would have embraced the saying, "It's better to burn out than fade away."

At least that's what I tell myself.

Leslie told me that she, David, and the rest of the team had talked at great length about the risks they took. They weren't naïve about their exploits. I don't know if any of them believed that it *would* happen, especially to someone so focused on safety, so fit, so prepared. But they all talked about danger—it's not something they squeezed into the backs of their minds.

But what they were doing wasn't just some game; it was everything. Through these conversations, David expressed his desire to be cremated. These were, apparently, ordinary things to discuss on the trails, during those blind night hikes and sweltering day rides.

The North Star

When the date for David's memorial service was set, Peyton was still on the road with the band, so I had to go it alone. My mother-in-law came to stay at the house and pet-sit. I gave her the more comfortable bed in our room and set myself up on the guest futon for the one night we would be staying together in the house before I flew to Houston.

While packing, I auditioned dresses for her. *Was all black morbid or appropriate? Was showing up in a color rude or too festive? Were pants wrong?* We settled on a simple wrap dress that was basically black with a white circle pattern, just to break it up a little. It was a poly-blend and would pack in a suitcase well. Practical and unfussy. David would have liked that aspect. I hoped it would be appropriate. I also threw in the only pair of black heels I had ever owned along with my curling iron, which I used irregularly, but considered the only tool in my arsenal that made my thick, straight hair do anything interesting or remotely formal.

Getting dressed for special occasions has always stressed me out. I've often felt woefully underdressed or just wrongly outfitted for weddings, job interviews, parties, and funerals, as I've remained a solidly jeans-and-t-shirt person since childhood. Because this was a memorial—not technically a funeral—and since David was such a laid-back guy, I wish I could have been more relaxed about it. But I was so uncomfortable in general that being prepared to put myself together helped my nerves a trifle.

It was just eight days after his body had been found. The idea of holding a service felt impossible. I hadn't even begun to process what had happened. Under the circumstances, thinking about dresses seemed ridiculous, but it gave me something else to focus on.

I still clung to the wish that we would be celebrating David's life in a park instead of a church—a place where his teammates, friends, colleagues, and family members could show up in shorts and t-shirts and maybe play Frisbee after the service or drink beers together in the shade. David had never liked being trapped indoors, despite his work as a radiologist. His natural habitat was a forest; he should have lived in a tree house. Another thing David and I had in common was that nature was the place where we felt connected to something bigger than ourselves, where we got inspiration, where we felt spiritual. I wanted to celebrate David outside, both for him and for myself.

I was also having big problems with God. It was hard to believe a benevolent spirit would rip away my beloved brother this way. And organized religion had bothered me since I was a teenager. Though I had spent my formative years in a close-knit, comfy Episcopal parish where my dad sang in the choir, by the time I was twelve (and questioning everything), the seemingly mindless repetitions of the same passages of scriptures and prayers struck me as empty gesturing. I started looking around at the congregation wondering if anyone was even thinking about the words they were saying, about what it meant to put a communion wafer in their mouths, about what they were doing when they made the sign of the cross. The only part of Sunday morning services that touched me was the offering of the peace, when attendees turned around to face each other, touch hands, give hugs, offer sentiments of comfort. Though I've always had a general sense of something spiritually larger than myself, from early on, I didn't have a name or a ritual for it. I just knew church wasn't it.

On top of all that, I knew definitively that David wasn't religious. I remembered vividly the year before, when I sat on a hard wooden pew next to David during Gran's funeral in St. Martin's Episcopal, both of us mildly wincing at the heavier Christian stuff, singing the hymns only because it seemed disrespectful not to (and because we feared Gran might smite us from above), going through the motions as we had been trained to as kids, saying our "amens" like talking parrots. Despite that, at some point during her funeral, David started to cry, and I put my arm around him. "I love you," I whispered as I hugged him from the side. It was the only time in my life I felt I could take care of him a little, when I was slightly more together emotionally, instead of the other way around. Afterward, he and I had talked about the parts of the event that felt phony, the passages that were read that sounded meaningless, the eulogies romanticizing her life.

He had been true to himself all along. The last thing I wanted for him was anything that felt false. But I was trying to accept that I couldn't be involved with organizing his memorial, especially from afar. Even if I had been in town, I wouldn't have had the fortitude to coordinate with the many members of our disjointed family. I hadn't always stayed in touch as closely as I could have. I didn't see everyone regularly, and no one understood why I hadn't moved back to Texas after college. Who was I to say what David would have wanted anyway? There were lots of people in Houston who had their own ideas and more capacity for planning at the time.

In the end, I slipped right back into the baby-of-the-family role, as I tended to do during family negotiations, conceding to others to avoid conflict. I felt insignificant in the scheme of things. Tommy and David were so close, after all. They were full brothers, not a halvsie like me. If anyone should have a say, it should have been Tommy. I figured he was likely too flattened with grief and exhaustion to entertain any ideas from his kid sister or do anything other than simply put one foot in front of the other.

David and Tommy's stepmother Sarah belonged to a Unitarian Church in a central location in Houston, so she booked it. In that religious space, foreign to me, we would be required, somehow, to say our goodbyes. I surrendered to the plan and turned my attention back to packing.

I chose just one piece of jewelry that held significance for me: a silver pendant formed in an open diamond shape, the four sides curved inward ever so slightly, making the gesture less angular than the symbol you would find on a playing card. A row of tiny diamond stones accented one of the sides. I had purchased this necklace with money Gran had willed me. The design had been marketed as "The North Star."

When David died in early September, the real North Star happened to be especially clear in the night sky. At the end of the street where Peyton and I lived was a forested hill. When I walked the dogs in the evenings, I looked up at that star nestled in the opening between the dark silhouettes of trees, prominently positioned there like a sparkling diamond in a prong setting.

It's tempting to believe you see signs when someone dies—and sometimes, to decide that he or she is appearing in a new form. The sense that the person must be *somewhere*, despite not being physically present, can be overwhelming. Mom had decided early on that a big yellow kingfisher who kept showing up on her street was David in the form of an exotic water bird. Because the North Star became so obvious to me immediately, I decided *it* was David, and that its flicker was him up there winking at me.

I've always loved stars, their shimmery appearance at night making a magical canopy drawn over the earth. In East Texas, where our family cabin stood, we had often walked down a long pier that jutted out over the lake after nightfall and lay on our backs, staring at all those shiny incredible dots, mesmerized by their patterns, not quite able to grasp the reality of their distance from us. Besides, I kept consoling myself by recalling the stars as "the headlights of angels."

David had always supported my quest for finding my own path, for being true to myself. He had also been dedicated to orienteering with a good old fashioned map and compass despite the advent of GPS during his recent years. He'd been the captain of his team, the leader, the guide. The North Star was a perfect symbol for him.

So, in my head, David was my North Star, as well as *the* North Star. I looked up at it every night, much as I had always looked up to my big brother. Wearing a symbol of this sparkling heavenly body around my neck was about as religious as I could get under the circumstances. It felt like a talisman for the occasion. I hoped it would provide some sense of security—or confidence or direction—as I traveled to a place I had never wanted to visit, a place where disparate family members were forced to interact under the worst of circumstances, where I would have to face the reality of what had occurred.

Personal Property

As I exited the plane and entered the overly air-conditioned terminal at George Bush Intercontinental Airport, I realized I was one of few passengers making an arrival instead of a departure. Like a salmon swimming upstream, I moved against a flood of people going in the opposite direction. The city wasn't under mandatory evacuation, but the threat of Hurricane Ike loomed large. Though downgraded from its original strength as a category four storm, Ike had been measured as having one-hundred-ten mile-per-hour winds, and it was tracking directly toward us. Many people were fleeing Houston just as I got in.

I met my mother outside of baggage claim. In front of her beloved big red Astrovan, she stood wearing jeans and a pale blue button-down shirt, rolled up at the sleeves. For as long as I could remember, Mom had permed her naturally straight hair, cropped it short, and added highlights to blend in the gray. From behind rimless glasses, her blue eyes looked tired. When she put her arms around me, I remembered that we are the short ones in the family, even if we don't share many other physical attributes. Her voice shaky, her head on my shoulder, she whispered into my long, dark hair, "It's okay. You're here now."

I couldn't imagine anything ever being okay again.

Mom and I drove over to David's house right after I arrived, theoretically to make sure it was prepped for hurricane-force weather. Mostly, I think we went because it was all we had left of him, and without saying so, we both badly wanted to touch something of his. I hopped out to punch the code into the keypad for his electronic fence, and as it mechanically retracted, a familiar-looking man came out to meet me, hand extended.

"I'm Shaun."

"I know who you are," I said, recognizing him from the many race photos. I ignored his outstretched hand and threw my arms around him. "My brother loved you so much," I muttered into his neck.

"He loved you so much too," Shaun said, both of us welling up.

Shaun escorted Mom and me into the house, and then politely retreated to the backyard, leaving us alone. It wasn't Mom's first time to visit the house since David's death, but it was mine. We used the entrance he always used, which was at the back of the house and took us through the garage into the kitchen. In the house where we grew up, we also rarely used the front door, instead entering through the garage into the kitchen. I hadn't thought of the parallel before, or how both were galley kitchens, long and narrow like hallways, or how in both settings, there was often a dog on the other side of the door.

Unlike our kitchen when we were kids, in David's, there was rarely much food on hand. I recalled bananas and cereal being the only mainstays, a quick breakfast to grab on his way out the door each day. Eaten standing up, just like on a race course. As I stood on the marble floor, I kept thinking about the wine opener I had sent him after my last visit, since we hadn't been able to find one after riffling through his many drawers, glad to have given him something, even something so basic, that he could use.

Off the kitchen, David's dining room, clearly never used for its original purpose, was filled to the rafters with mountain bikes, bike parts, and bike tools. Wheels angled up toward the chandelier, and skeletal frames draped over the table. The array, his workshop, looked like a crazy site-specific sculpture installation.

I walked through the other eerily quiet rooms slowly, viewing everything with an odd kind of distance, as if the items were in a cold museum instead of a home where I had comfortably stayed just the previous year.

I re-started my tour in David's bedroom. Someone had said there were pictures of me by his bed, but they had already been moved by the time I got there. I lay down and pressed my face into his pillows, desperately hoping there might be a lingering trace of his smell. I breathed in over and over again, practically hyperventilating, but couldn't capture anything. They were probably clean sheets—until I started crying all over them.

"I know," a voice from the doorway spoke, and I turned to find David's sweetheart, Cheryl, standing there in shorts and a t-shirt without her hair done, sans make-up, looking so unlike the glamorous woman I'd met over dinner the year before. "I tried it too."

It was good to hug another confessed pillow-huffer. And good to see her there. Absorbed in my own shock after getting the news, I hadn't given much thought to Cheryl, but now I remembered she was one of the last people to see David, having gone to Colorado on that very trip with him along with her eight-year-old daughter and our seven-year-old nephew, both of whom worshipped my brother just the way I had growing up.

I kept poking around: I found funny toe-socks in the drawer in his bedroom closet and wondered if they kept his feet warm during races or if they were a novelty. I touched his hanging shirts, running my hand along the fabrics. Lots of them still had their tags on, but others were quite well-loved; a crisp, striped button-down from Barney's hung right next to a worn green flannel. Many size-twelve shoes were neatly lined up beneath—probably his house cleaner's doing, as he was never so tidy. These were his doctor's shoes, loafers and Oxfords, nicely shined. Next to them were the black snakeskin cowboy boots he wore for dressy occasions.

It felt wrong to be going through David's things. But privacy is over when you're dead. And this was more than nosiness; we needed to be with his possessions if we couldn't be with him.

The double-wide closet across from his bed opened to all hunting clothes. He had an entire wardrobe of camouflage in there: pants, jackets, body suits, caps, gloves, hats. Another closet held ammunition—a whole closet! The safe in the living room had apparently been full of guns—many more than I knew—but Tommy had already gone through it and taken them. I had conveniently forgotten how much hunting was a part of David's life. He, Tommy, and their dad had always hunted, and I had always taken issue with it. A tender-hearted animal lover, I bristled at the idea of shooting serene grazing does from a deer blind and knocking ducks out of the sky mid-flight for sport. The fact that they generally processed and ate their kill was a minor consolation. I was tired of hearing excuses about how the deer were overpopulating areas that humans had made crowded for them and trying futilely to express the latter point.

Another closet, this time in the workout room, which merely held a weight bench, was jammed with so many camping supplies the door wouldn't properly close. For no good reason—other than perhaps owning something his warm, alive body had once been in—I decided I had to have his purple and black, down sleeping bag. I don't camp, but it's jammed in *my* closet now, and I like having it there.

Mom dug through plastic DVD boxes in the living room.

"What are you doing?" I asked.

"Making sure there isn't any porn here." I guessed she meant so that it could be thrown out so no one else found it? "But I only found a bunch of cycling videos."

"That *was* his porn," I replied seriously, wishing she hadn't provoked the image of writhing naked bodies. I switched gears to the year before when David animatedly explained time trials to me while we watched his enormous TV as one rider after another, clad in colorful spandex, tested their speed on bikes.

Glass cases in the living room were stuffed with huge quantities of glittering gold trophies, plaques, commemorative belt buckles, and medals of all size, red and blue ribbons, photos, and knickknacks, all scattered inside rather than carefully displayed. Later, other racers told me he had given many of his prizes away, so it was incredible how many were left, though his treatment of them spoke volumes about how little they mattered to him.

Only a few dozen books graced the shelves—many that were recognizable as gifts from Mom and me—a lot of them clearly unread as proven by their pristine, unbroken spines. They were about mountains and fearlessness and bicycles and deserts and survival in the wilderness. I thought we had chosen pretty well, but David had obviously been too busy doing the real thing to read about it.

Stacks of random paperwork, never filed, sat on his desk, the floor of the guest room, the kitchen counter. Mostly bills and lists. We went through all of it anyway because no one had yet found a will.

The den, hidden behind two sliding doors, was tidy, clearly rather unvisited, unlived in, and as creepy as I recalled. Other than a fireplace he never lit and two leather couches on which no one ever sat, the room simply housed hunting souvenirs. Dark wooden panels flanked the room, and from them sprung a near forest's worth of taxidermied creatures: ducks flew off the walls, deer walked through them as if by magic, a bobcat was suspended in a hiss, a noble looking elk craned his neck, and a whole black bear stood up ominously in the corner, its face stuck in a frozen snarl. Lots of brittle-looking pale-grey deer antlers were littered around, which at least had been shed instead of harvested. That room had always seemed to me like a scene from a David Lynch film, freakishly out of place for a loving person whose professional job was to save lives. I couldn't ever see these items as something to revere; they were simply proof of killing, of power and control—carcasses animated grotesquely into shapes to mimic the living.

The bathroom cabinet, where I retreated, held dozens of samples of prescription drugs, mostly expired. But there was also a full bottle of Hydrocodone, prescribed to him within the year, though for what I didn't know. I pocketed four of the white tablets, sneaking like a little kid, thinking they might come in handy if I needed to take the edge off. Because I was edgy like I'd never been before. In a drawer of the washstand, I found the small silver box I had had engraved with David's initials, DBB, a Christmas present from a few years back. It was empty. Later, it would sit on my dresser holding a portion of his ashes, having finally found its purpose.

What I didn't find that day, and never found, was David's big mouth bass. Of all the trophies in his life, the fish was the only one that mattered to me because I knew how he treasured it.

My dad, his step-father, enjoyed repeating the story of how, as a teenager, David went out fishing by himself on the lake in East Texas and came back to the cabin triumphantly yelling about a stunningly large bass he'd hauled in. My dad was duly impressed with the catch, and was the one who introduced my brother to taxidermy that day. The simple wooden plaque with the bass mounted on it had traveled with my brother back and forth to multiple houses, to college and med school, to his residency in Kansas City, and to this one-story sprawling home. Its fins and the lip of its gaping mouth had chipped from all the handling. But it was nowhere to be found, just like my brother.

As we were leaving, exiting through the garage, we found more shoes in an enormous pile between the washing machine and a side wall: sandals, hiking boots, wet shoes, flip-flops, and a heap of dozens of pairs of sneakers in a rainbow of colors. So many shoes, we didn't know where to begin.

And such big feet.

The Salesman

Mom and I next stopped over to see Tommy at his house, which was close to her place. I had felt sick to my stomach for days, imagining the weight of his sadness, having been so close to David since the day he was born—wondering how he would manage without his big bro. I wanted to bring him comfort or bridge the gap between us through our shared grief, but I knew this wasn't likely to happen. We weren't accustomed to being vulnerable around each other, and Tommy, who often behaved like a professional salesman even around me, was accustomed to putting on a good face.

As soon as we walked in, Mom and I hugged my sister-in-law Alison and their kids. I then grabbed my tall brother, squeezing him hard, attempting to demonstrate through physical sensation what I couldn't communicate in words. He quickly extracted himself and settled into a chair behind a large heavy wooden desk in his home office, just off the entryway, as if we had arrived for a business meeting. As usual, he seemed confident and secure. I never knew if his demeanor was partly a front, but I wanted so badly to fall apart with him, to connect that way. He wouldn't let his guard down.

I settled on the couch, and someone handed me David's laptop—or I picked it up—I can't remember. But somehow it arrived on my trembling lap, open. I found myself without hesitation rifling through his folder of pictures, as if investigating, unsure of what I was looking for or how I ended up in his personal files.

And there it was, a selfie, before we called them that—or at least before "selfie" was added to the dictionary. Part of David's extended left arm is in the frame, draped in a rust orange, long-sleeved shirt, leading to his broad shoulder and grinning face. It was the first photo I ever saw where he was showing his age: soft grey hairs peppered his bushy eyebrows and his beard, which was more like a heavy five o'clock shadow, and lines crinkled around his eyes and on his brow. His white cap bore the Primal Quest logo—I recognized it through the lenses of his sunglasses, which were perched on the brim, his usual outdoor look. In the background, expansive blue sky shot through with airy wisps of clouds hovered above a jagged ridgeline of crumbly-looking sand-colored rocks. A barren landscape, but one with a striking view, which clearly delighted him. It looked precisely like the place described to me on Little Bear, under which his body was discovered.

"When was this taken?" I asked the room in general.

Everyone was talking amongst themselves, and no one responded to me.

I stared into the computer screen as if through a window into the recent past. I felt it might be the last photo of my brother. I loved knowing that he took this picture of himself, thinking that it could have been the record of one of his final moments, a final feeling—and because he is so ecstatic inside the frame, it made things ever-so-slightly better.

It was where he wanted to be.

I started to cry. Already perhaps attempting to step into the oldest brother role and console me, Tommy said, "What can I give you to make you feel better?" He had David's backpack at his side and reached into it. "Do you want his iPod? You love music. I probably don't even know any of these bands. Here, take it."

I couldn't believe he was making such an offering; it was a gesture of unusual generosity. I grabbed the piece of plastic like it was gold, before he could change his mind, and started scrolling through David's songs.

At some point, a cell phone rang, and he answered it with his full name, "This is Tom Boyd."

I assumed it would be a work call, maybe because of how formally he answered, which I had heard dozens of times. Tommy was a mortgage broker. It must be someone needing loan assistance. While he talked and I overheard the one-sided conversation, I realized that the phone he had answered was not his—it was David's. And he was speaking to someone on the other end who had called *for* David, which meant—as I listened in horror—that I had to overhear Tommy telling the caller why David wasn't answering.

Who had given him this job, the worst job anyone could have? Did he take it, not knowing what else to do? During the visit, maybe an hour long, I heard him unflinchingly tell the gruesome story more than once.

Storm Surge

When we got to Mom's at last, instead of preparing mentally or otherwise for David's memorial service, scheduled for just two days out, we prepped her house for the hurricane, which would be making landfall the following day. I had been lucky to get in before the airport shut down.

The modest three-bedroom ranch-style home Mom bought when I was twelve, likely built in the 1950s, was swiftly becoming the exception of house styles in the area, as they were regularly being bulldozed to make way for outsized stucco "mansionettes" built astonishingly close to property lines. Bellaire, a small sub-city inside Houston, had become a more and more desirable location as Houston boomed and sprawled. Her carefully landscaped backyard had recently been cast in shadow by a three-story house built just behind her back fence, and she was cranky about it.

I helped my mother move her planters of nasturtiums, begonias, and herbs; the many bird feeders she lovingly filled each day; the patio umbrella and chairs, and anything else not anchored to the ground, other than the patio table, which was too heavy for us to lift, from the deck into the garage. We drilled sheets of plywood against the biggest windows, taped the smaller ones, filled bottles of water, checked batteries in flashlights. It was a routine I hadn't practiced in many years, but it came back to me, and I worked as if on autopilot, uncomplaining, unlike the many times I had arrived home just in time to do a list of chores she'd planned. Despite what we were able to do together, I couldn't help but think about how helpful David would have been right then, with his strong hands and ability to stay calm under duress.

The following night was, absurdly, Mom's birthday, and I was proud of my advance planning, having sent gifts ahead of time, purchased before I was undone by our mutual loss. In the kitchen, she opened them while we ate leftover sandwiches a friend had brought by the day before. Unceremonious, but better than nothing, considering the circumstances. When the storm blew in later, instead of enjoying a movie we watched scenes of the drama unfolding on The Weather Channel as if they were happening in another city far away. Then the electricity abruptly went out and the clamor and brightness of the TV cut off with it, casting us into darkness.

The physical exertion of the day helped me fall asleep despite the turmoil of my brain, but in the middle of the night, my mother shook me awake.

"Mom, what's wrong?" I could just make out her face peering over me.

"I'm sorry, but the weather is getting really bad," she whispered, even though we were the only ones there. "I don't want you sleeping next to the window." The window in question had been taped, but I wanted to do whatever she asked to make her feel safe.

I followed her into the hallway where she had made a palette of sleeping bags and pillows to cushion the hardwood floor in the small space between five rooms. We huddled close in the dark for hours, listening to news reports on an old, tinny transistor radio, shifting its antenna occasionally for better reception. A woman described windows shattering in the skyscrapers downtown. Another reporter gave an account of storm drains spilling over, of tree branches snapping, and electrical lines coming down. All we could see from our soft bunker were bursts of poisonous-looking green lightning flashing into the living room just beyond us, somehow still brightly coming through the blinds and the tape.

Wind encircled the house, its volume escalating each hour. Rain pounded the wooden siding at angles, loud as hail. Off and on, we dozed, woken occasionally by the sound of something unknown breaking outside.

"This feels like being in the The Wizard of Oz," I said. As if we'd be swept up in a surreal vortex and dropped who knew where.

In the morning, I opened the front door cautiously. Overnight, life had gone from simple sadness to chaos. Mom's front yard had turned into marshland it was so saturated with rain. Sticks, branches, and leaves were scattered everywhere. The crossed red street sign with white lettering, along with part of its metal post, once securely anchored on the corner a dozen houses away, had landed right in front of her driveway and lay like a broken body.

The city was all but shut down. Power was a precious commodity. Streets were closed to accommodate strewn detritus. David's memorial would have to be delayed for a week. I had intended to be away for exactly four days—a long weekend—the amount of time I knew I could visit family comfortably before we started getting on each other's nerves. The disruption of Ike meant being there a minimum of seven additional days. My boss was sympathetic and accommodating, but I felt marooned and stressed.

I took solace in cleaning up Mom's yard. The strenuous labor of breaking up tree limbs, raking mounds of soggy leaves, and moving heavy garbage bags to the curb in the thickly humid air kept the real pain at bay. Missing Peyton, I wore my Silver Jews t-shirt as I hauled trash. Peyton and I talked only a little, as he was busy and my cell phone battery constantly needed recharging.

It was hard to get around town, so Mom and I were each other's sole company for days. When we finally made it out, we stood in lines wrapped around whole parking lots just to buy a couple of bags of ice for our diminishing perishables. At night, we cooked simple meals on her gas stove and ate oddly romantically by candlelight at her round dining room table where we had celebrated all those Christmases together. David always sat on the old day bed positioned at one end instead of a chair. He liked to lie back after Mom's hearty, delicious meals, hands clasped together over his full belly, eyes closed and a soft smirk on his face. I missed him there already.

Before bed most nights, Mom and I would take simultaneous baths in the dark, one of us in each of her two bathrooms, keeping the doors open so that we could listen to Willie Nelson croon from the boom box positioned in the room between. His voice had been a soothing sound since my childhood when Mom first played his songs for me. For days, I slept in my underwear on top of the sheets because it was so hot without the air conditioning. Opening the windows didn't help because even at night, temperatures were in the high eighties and the air was soggy with humidity.

Each morning, we would call around to see if anyone had gotten power back. When I checked in with Tommy, he said, "It's like Dave's trying to keep us from having a funeral for him." The idea that our brother was attempting to derail our efforts from the Great Beyond made us laugh. But only for a minute.

Playlist

I spent the next week compulsively shuffling through the 860 tracks on David's iPod. I knew he liked energetic music for motivation during workouts, during a run, or while mountain biking—songs he would "hammer" to, an expression he and his teammates used, which I translated to mean pushing hard, giving it their all. David had two different playlists called "On the Go."

He loved Nickelback, The Offspring, and Staind, which always cracked me up. An admitted music snob, I had taken every opportunity to steer him toward options I found more palatable and still rocking—bands that had the same kind of driving energy, like Queens of the Stone Age and Helmet. An equal-opportunity music-lover, he happily adopted them. I was pleased to find the CD I had given him the past Christmas had been added to his iPod.

I always knew his musical taste was eclectic but was still surprised at the variety. He had more '80s and '90s bands in there than I ever imagined. How did we miss talking about our mutual love of The Cocteau Twins, The Psychedelic Furs, Modern English, and Nine Inch Nails? I had no idea. And I'm pretty sure he made fun of me for loving Duran Duran growing up. I laughed to myself; now he was busted.

There were a few more cringe-worthy artists: Brooks and Dunn, The Goo Goo Dolls. *Really, David? Bon Jovi?* I would have given him such crap. If he were there. Perhaps most incongruous was Sarah McLachlan among the mix. Fascinating to me. A portrait of my musical taste would be far less eclectic.

I thought about how the iPod was with him on that last day. Maybe the ear buds were still in his ears. Was he listening to something right at that moment? Which song was it? Could he hear it?

Was there a soundtrack to that fall?

Travel Plans

Something about death can make people behave in atypical ways. The rules change, at least temporarily. Once unimaginable combinations of people—people who hadn't been on speaking terms for ages or never even intended to meet again at all—now gathered graciously, a positive disruption that death, apparently, can make possible.

I was surprised that Mom had accepted an invitation to a dinner party at David's dad Charles' and stepmother Sarah's house along with many of their family members who had come to town for the memorial service. It had to have been decades since my mother had spoken to her ex. In their still-dark, post-hurricane house, Mom sat in the living room chatting away with veritable strangers, drinking the wine that was offered, and engaging in a warm, open way that filled me with optimism. Among candle-light and headlamps, I loved the experience of overhearing stories about my brother while glasses clinked, and seeing my mother at ease in the company of those she hadn't seen in ages.

I embraced moments when family members came together, so rare in my upbringing, as it seemed people were constantly being split up. I basked in the glow of my splintered family tree being knitted together for one precious evening; the divorce-torn little girl in me delighted by the occasion. It made sense that David, who had so often held disparate pieces of our family together, had made this happen.

A few days later, Mom and I joined Charles and Sarah at the funeral home. We were swiftly ushered into a small parlor plastered with too-frilly wallpaper, the ornate flowers adorning it seeming to suck up all the oxygen in the room. I noticed Kleenex boxes on every table, every side table and shelf, ready for catching tears. Formal gilt chairs and sofa, more befitting a French mansion than this place, flanked the walls, entirely unwelcoming. So, I stood, my tight skirt painfully pinching my waist, along with several family members, none of us speaking.

After what felt like hours but was surely less than one, a funeral director appeared in the doorway and handed us a box the size of which might have held a child's pair of shoes.

Sarah said quickly, "That's not *him*." And we all understood what she meant. How could someone we loved for decades, with such enormous presence in our lives, be reduced to this? All those atoms, organs, blood, bones, and cells that used to sleep under the stars; the muscles he built, the tendons he stretched, the teeth he took such good care of (always flossing, probably even in the desert), his Lasik-perfected eyes, his studied and compassionate radiologist's hands, his full head of hair just barely starting to gray, his pierced heart, and his amazing brain—were dust.

We all looked down at the black plastic box balanced in our hands in the mystified way someone might stare at a sinkhole that appeared in the ground overnight with no explanation.

David was an avid traveler, fearless and curious, in awe of the natural world. He had gone as far as Australia for competition with his adventure racing team and to Greenland just for sight-seeing. Much of Mexico and South America had been covered, some of it by foot and bike, parts of it by boat. His Spanish was adequate, and he was famously good at making friends with anyone because of his easygoing demeanor.

I could imagine him ordering food in a Spanish-speaking country the way he had for us at a local taqueria: "Dos tacos con huevos y chorizo con queso, por favor," he would say, with a distinctly Texan accent while holding up two fingers and smiling, reinforcing the request for two plates while also seeming to say, "Peace."

David delighted me with his stories of traversing the world. I learned about the landscape of Tasmania, with its lush greenery and soaring rocky cliffs. He showed me photos of himself squatting next to kangaroos, petting them as if they were dogs, and standing knee-deep in swamps with his teammates. For the first time, I saw that Tasmanian devils were nothing like the horrible, blathering Looney Toons character, but rather tenaciously cute animals.

"We were canoeing at night in Louisiana in this swamp," I remember him telling me once. "Of course we couldn't really see. We were imagining alligators all around us and we were dog-tired, but we had to keep going so we didn't lose pace. So, I taught them the Kookaburra song. It kept us awake and made us paddle really steadily because of the rhythm." This was a song we had sung with our parents during car trips growing up, splitting into rounds and repeating the lyrics over and over: "Kookaburra sits in the old gum tree, merry merry king of the bush is he, laugh Kookaburra, laugh Kookaburra, gay our lives must be."

I envisioned my brother running through the sun-scorched red dirt of Moab, Utah, climbing its snow-covered mountain faces, and finishing a ropes course in Arches National Park. He told me about tromping through snow in Montana, showed me photos of himself bundled in a down jacket and wool hat in Iceland. From the selfie on top of the mountains in Colorado, I had seen his joy. After being born and raised at sea level, I wasn't surprised that elevation was so thrilling to him, his desire to stand on top of the world and see all there was to see, overwhelming.

In honor of my brother's love of travel, there was a plan for his ashes to travel. Friends and family were going to take pieces of him with them to both everyday and exotic places. Everyone who knew him agreed that it didn't make any sense for a guy with such wanderlust to be stuck in one spot for all eternity. The idea was that his final resting place would be all over the globe, rather than one location.

I was on board philosophically. The process of actually divvying up my brother's ashes, however, turned out to be rather surreal.

My mother and I drove from the funeral parlor with the box, unceremoniously, straight to Target, in hopes of finding some appropriate containers. She and I had been given this responsibility, or honor, depending on how you looked at it.

David's remains rested on my lap as I sat in the passenger seat. It was heavy, considering. Clearly not your everyday ashes from a wood fire. Having never held such a thing, the sensation was surprising. While the package was ridiculously small for such a big person and personality, it was dense. The idea that my brother had been compressed into a parcel I could hold in my hands was hard to reconcile. Leaving it unattended in the car while we shopped was just as strange and seemed like a crime of negligence, but we did it anyway because walking around with that black plastic box would have been even weirder.

Mom and I stood in the fluorescently lit aisles considering proper receptacles in which loved ones could carry portions of ashes. Ziplock baggies were practical but seemed tasteless. A paper box wasn't secure. Tins might be good. Standing there considering options in the gift-wrapping section among the brightly colored papers, balloons, and bags, I began wishing for a store that just carried tiny urns.

"Should we just buy a few of everything?" I asked her. I wanted to get out of there and go home to take off my stupid skirt.

"Okay. Anything else you need while we're here?" Ever practical, on that day she dismayed me.

"Um, no."

After our Target shopping spree, Mom, Sarah, and I reassembled at the Unitarian church where we had agreed to hold the service. There we were taking on the bizarre job of making parcels out of what was left of my brother. The church building housed a cozy library on its second floor, with a long, rectangular table surrounded by chairs, which seemed suitable for the task of ash division, if there is such a place. Mom and I sat on one side and Sarah and the minister on the other. While he didn't directly participate in the project at hand, his third-party company was pacifying.

Reverend Edmiston-Lange was a relaxed and likeable guy, with a hippie beard and unassuming personality. As we worked, he asked about David in gentle, inquisitive ways. I learned later how closely he had listened. When he later delivered the eulogy,

I would be deeply grateful for his attempts to understand the unique person my brother was.

Attempting to figure out a good process for packaging, I configured a small piece of paper into a little funnel and portioned out David's remains like drugs into dime bags. There were many parcels to make; many people would want a pinch. He had a full brother and several other half-siblings like me, along with friends, colleagues, teammates, and cousins. By the end of the day, we would end up using our entire motley assortment of gathered receptacles.

His teammate Shaun had bravely and movingly announced that he would finish what David started; he would take ashes with him as he scaled the remaining fourteen of the fourteeners that my brother had not lived to conquer. Sarah had found the ideal containers for this purpose: waterproof match holders from REI. She bought exactly fourteen of these compact vessels, one for each peak David hadn't reached. We were duly impressed with her clarity and choice.

As I poured, I couldn't help sifting a little in my fingers, as if touching all that was left of my big brother would reconnect me to him. I discovered startling white chunks, clearly from bones or teeth, something that had not fully broken down in the fire. I ran across a little metal staple in the grey, chalky material and brought it to their attention, thinking it was an unintentional thing not meant to be in there, like maybe some papers accidentally ended up in the furnace?

"Must be from his vasectomy," Sarah said matter-of-factly.

"What?"

"Oh, yeah. He had the procedure done a few years ago."

Why I thought I would, or should, know this intimate detail was unclear. But why did she? This teeny metal piece had survived the burning, totally intact, and reminded me of the conversation he and I had had the year before about our mutual lack of interest in having children.

Mom and Sarah wondered aloud if the parcels needed labeling of some sort—as if someone might later think, *Hmmm, I wonder whose ashes these are?* The graphic designer in me regretted not being able to create a special tag or sticker. We ended up using permanent markers to write "David Brooks Boyd 1961-2008" on the larger packages or just "DBB" on the smaller ones. The informality felt appropriate for him.

We gave Sarah a number of them to take to her family members, and we took a few. I had the fourteen REI tubes in their own box, ready to bestow upon Shaun.

In Pictures

With the memorial service pushed back an entire week, Mom and I took the opportunity to work on a corkboard collage of pictures of David to display at the reception. We went through veritable mountains of her old photographs, musing, crying, and laughing as we culled. In the first paper packets we opened were black and white shots of him as a toddler and young boy in the 1960s: in a highchair, eating, holding his baby brother on his lap, posed for a studio portrait, petting a white rabbit in the backyard. In every one, he showed the classic toothy grin he'd flashed throughout his life.

"Geez, was he never not cute?" I asked.

"Well, I always thought he was cute," she said. But then she revealed photographic evidence of the brief time, maybe ages twelve to fourteen, during which David wasn't totally adorable—when he had glasses, braces, and long hair at the same time. It was hilarious that even though he'd turned out to be such a lady-killer, he did have this awkward period.

"It seems kind of mean to put these up," I said, giggling. "Well, maybe just one, for historical accuracy." I reveled in being able to review his life this way and having a role in designing the display.

We moved on chronologically through her meticulously organized boxes of envelopes and arrived at those in which I finally came on the scene; from there, all of the images were in color. A favorite was of Tommy, David, and me lying on the living room floor, our heads resting on pillows pulled from the couch. My brothers are covered by a green and navy-blue afghan, and I'm kept warm by my blue baby blanket, the one that I loved so much it earned me another boy nickname, Linus. My brothers are probably watching TV, but I am watching the camera. David's right arm is behind his head and his left is around me, holding me close. In it, he is in his awkward physical phase, but I added this one too, pushing thumbtacks carefully around the edges.

We cracked up at a shot of the three of us dancing around a sombrero on the den floor. I am naked with a pink protruding belly, Tommy is wearing a YMCA t-shirt and ball cap, and David has a second sombrero on his head. The décor is so painfully 1970s: an olive-green shag carpet is underfoot, two couches with alarmingly gaudy blue and green plaid patterns frame our dance floor, the windows are dressed in bamboo blinds, and a lamp with a woven brown flower-shaped shade hangs from the ceiling on a big gold-link chain. The setting of my childhood came flooding back.

In my favorite early image of all three of us, I am the meat in a brother sandwich, snuggly situated between them on the floor. At two, wearing a red smock dress, I sit with legs out straight, smiling toward the photographer, likely Dad. Tommy and David lie on their bellies, propped on their elbows, staring at, smiling at, me.

As David aged photographically, he evolved into the handsome doctor and outdoor adventurer we remembered best. In an underwater picture, he dove through blue depths like some Jacques Cousteau, in full scuba gear, grabbing the big orange legs of a crab. He stood in front of a rusted-out shipwreck with feet firmly apart, flippers in one hand, snorkel in the other, and a knife strapped to his calf. He held trophies from the sea in front of his bare, muscular chest: an enormous fish, a squirming eel, a lobster with foot-long antennae.

David's life in pictures included images of him with multiple medals hanging around his neck after a triathlon; receiving his degree from the University of Texas in a burnt orange cap and gown; wearing camouflage in front of a boat draped with the limp carcasses of ducks from a recent hunt; standing in a line with his medical school buddies, each of them in t-shirts and shorts holding red Solo cups, presumably full of beer, and laughing. In a portrait of David among his radiology group members dressed in suits, he is the only one in scrubs and sneakers. There were also images of him in a tux at Tommy and Alison's wedding and others of him in a suit at mine and Peyton's, proving he cleaned up good too. At the end, I added one from the Primal Quest trip that Glenn had taken just a couple of months before in which David looks seriously into the camera while ascending a ridge, calf muscles bulging.

There were far too many good ones for the corkboard. I made sure I was present and that important family vacations were documented, but we edited out ones with his dad and my dad, as this was Mom's board, and it seemed fair to let her curate these memories.

Strange Magic

The weather delay meant that, in another uncanny alignment, Peyton would be crossing paths with me again during his weeks-long tour. The band was scheduled to play Houston a few days before the rescheduled memorial date. I missed him so much—my touchstone to normalcy—and had been wearing my Silver Jews t-shirt every night to sleep in. The tee was a soft, bright blue one with the handwritten word, *niteclub*, and a line drawing of an outsized floating dog-like animal connected to the roof of the night club by a string, like an homage to the pig balloon from Pink Floyd's *The Wall* tour. David Berman, the Silver Jews' song-writer and band leader was also the illustrator. That was the tee I'd been presented with the night in Northampton before the phone call that would change my life. The tee I wore during that time suspended between what had been and what would be.

Peyton flew from New Orleans ahead of his bandmates who were driving over in their van, so he could have a full day with me. Which meant with me and Mom, of course, and the three of us celebrated his arrival by eating Grand Slam plates at the Denny's near the airport, which was mobbed because it was one of the only restaurants open.

Even though most buildings were without power, including the originally slated club, a venue nearby was bright with electricity, and its owner agreed to host the show. A curfew was still in place after the hurricane, so the concert was rescheduled to start early. I invited my mother and David's teammates, Patti and Shaun, to join me, the four of us an improbable group at a rock show.

After having dinner together, we walked over to Walter's on Washington, near the arts district. "We're on the list," I proclaimed at the door and waltzed in with my odd little crew. Right away, I ran into a high school friend I hadn't seen in a couple of years, but whom I remembered being a huge Silver Jews fan, and he slapped me back to reality.

"What are *you* doing here?" Troy asked.

In the midst of reuniting with Peyton and the band, I had forgotten my interloper status in the city and had to relay the details about David to him quickly and without breaking down, which I didn't want to do. Within a few minutes of the show starting, Shaun bought everyone a round of beers, and we were smiling and tapping our toes.

"How do you hold this and clap?" Mom asked at the end of a song, clutching her red plastic beer cup. I demonstrated by biting the rim and suspending mine from my teeth as I put my hands together, and she imitated me, both of us chuckling and nearly spilling. Never did I think I'd be drinking with my mother in the back of a dingy club while my talented husband and his friends serenaded us. It was not her scene, to say the least—going to the ballet was her jam—but she embraced the moment.

I couldn't have dreamed up a scenario in which Mom, David's best friends, Peyton, and a dear high school buddy would ever have been in the same room together, much less all of us swaying together to music, beer cups clenched in our teeth. The show ended up being a special event for Houston in general, as it provided a rare opportunity for people to get out of their broken and dark houses post-Ike and enjoy the distraction of entertainment.

"I can't imagine any show I'd rather do right now," said David Berman from the stage that night.

What an odd gift, that lovely surprise congregation. This was strange magic, an alchemy borne of sudden death and natural disaster, a happy collision offsetting the pain that had brought us there.

Memorial(s)

Sarah called me a couple of days before the rescheduled service was to take place. She told me that my sister-in-law Alison had chosen a passage from *The Little Prince* for the service and wanted me to read it. I was put off. Why would I read something I hadn't selected? Why didn't she call me herself? What was this passage anyway? I was irritated because I wanted to do my own thing, and I didn't know why Alison had any say. I even knew she was nearly my ex-sister-in-law; that summer, David had told me that she and Tommy were getting divorced.

"You're kidding!" I had said with genuine shock.

"Oh, it's been a long time coming," he said. "You just haven't been around to see it." It stung that I didn't know what was going on in my brother's marriage because I was so removed, and I felt the same tug of jealousy at their closeness that I had all my life. I was just the kid sister after all.

I certainly wanted a part in the memorial. So, I agreed to Alison's reading, but only in exchange for my own opportunity to read a short piece about David I had drafted on the plane. I edited the piece by hand in a small notebook while sitting on the bed in the guest room at Mom's, the room where David had stayed when visiting from medical school in Galveston or his following residency in Kansas City.

When the morning of the memorial finally arrived, after days of waiting and days of enduring, the simple acts of bathing, dressing, and applying a little mascara seemed like a lot of effort. Having lugged the curling iron in my suitcase was pointless, I could now see. There was still no electricity to power vanity, and after everything, it felt silly anyway. I ditched stockings because of the humidity, but the dress was comfortable and didn't need ironing—it had been a solid choice. I looked in the bathroom mirror, the same one I had used to primp during middle and high school, hung the North Star pendant around my neck, and said to my flat hair, "Fuck it." I was as ready as I was going to be.

Mom and I made the short drive from her neighborhood to the church. I walked in that bright and clear Saturday morning feeling more like an attendee than a participant, as I didn't know the program schedule or whom exactly I would see. Why hadn't Sarah told us what to expect or asked for our input beyond one reading? And why hadn't we asked for details? At least my attire seemed suitable. As I looked around the church, there were lots of women in dark dresses. Still, I was nervously sweating under mine while they looked cool.

In the high-ceilinged foyer, guests were being handed orange rubber wristbands. Shaun and other members of team MOAT had designed them to match the color of David's special mountain bike, the one he rode on his last day. On each bracelet, the letters "WWDBD" were debossed in the plastic.

What Would Dave Boyd Do? An expression twisted from *What Would Jesus Do?*, the personal motto of evangelical Christians. If thinking my brother was a super-hero all my life wasn't hyperbolic enough, here his teammates were now likening him to a savior.

As I tentatively walked into the sanctuary, I eyed the bright orange bike propped on the altar in the place one might have expected a coffin. It hadn't crossed my mind what would be there, if anything. We had already divided David's ashes, so there wasn't even an urn to use. The bicycle, with no rider, was eerie. Again, I wondered who had made these decisions without us. But once I got used to it, I liked it up there as a stand-in for him, its flaming color making the tone more celebratory than morbid—it was so *him.*

Tommy, red-faced and looking tight in his suit, encouraged me to sit in the front pew with him and his kids, which felt good. But sitting with them and Alison plus Charles and Sarah, who were also in the first pew, instead of with Mom, felt vaguely disloyal. Navigating family alliances had long been a tricky issue for me. I was torn, but chose to be with my brother, relegating Mom to sitting with David's girlfriend Cheryl a couple of rows back. I settled in next to my five-year-old niece, Emily, who squirmed uncomfortably. Long before the service officially began, she started sobbing and repeated miserably the words we all wanted to say, "I want Uncle Dave, I want Uncle Dave." Her flowered dress was bunched up in back and the bow in her soft blonde hair was askew. I touched her flushed cheek and responded the only way I could, "I know."

Her brother Christopher, my nephew who had been in Colorado with David the day before he died, looked much older than his seven years with his pink and swollen downcast eyes. What an experience for such a young boy. Looking at him, I worried I might completely lose my tenuous composure.

After the minister delivered a short greeting, a song began to play over the sound system. I looked at my program, and it read, *Music for Biking: "Rise Today," Alter Bridge.* I had never heard anything more incongruous in a church than this modern rock song. I stifled a laugh, not what I thought I'd be doing in church, especially then. When the last chord played, the reverend called my name. Without so much as glancing at Alison, lest my annoyance show, I carefully ascended the steps in my heels, stood in front of the pulpit, and nervously started reading the passage I had been assigned, but had not even glanced at, much less practiced.

The little prince met the fox for the first time and wanted to play.

"'I cannot play with you,' the fox said. 'I am not tamed.'"

What is this? I thought. *And where is it going?* Did David even like *The Little Prince*? It had been years since I had read it.

"'Ah! Please excuse me,' said the little prince. But after some thought, he added: 'What does that mean—"tame"?'"

"'It is an act too often neglected,' said the fox. 'It means to establish ties.'"

I refused to look up at the congregation. I was embarrassed imagining that all of these people would think I had chosen this reading. But I pushed on because it was too late to turn back:

The fox explained how his life of hunting chickens and running from men was dull and repetitive, and the way all chickens and all men were the same to him. He told the little prince how much it would mean to know someone distinctly, to recognize a footfall different from the men, one that would beckon rather than terrify him.

"'If you tame me, it will be as if the sun came to shine on my life.'"

The fox described the wheat fields nearby and how, not being a bread eater, he had never had any use for them. But they were the same golden color as the little prince's blonde hair.

"'Think how wonderful that will be when you have tamed me!' the fox said. 'The grain, which is also golden, will bring me back the thought of you. And I shall love to listen to the wind in the wheat …'"

I didn't realize until reaching the end that the reading was a deeply meaningful choice. David was our little prince and we— all of us in that room—were the foxes he had tamed. We, who would forever be buoyed by the sight of metaphorical wheat fields because of his absence. Alison wasn't an idiot, after all. The surprise of it made me suddenly choke up, and I hurried back to my seat.

While I caught my breath, the minister delivered a surprisingly moving eulogy, giving every impression he had actually known David, though he had not. (I remembered his gentle prying during the ashes project a few days before.) A couple of people I didn't know, but who were clearly friends of my brother, played and sang Sarah McLachlan's "Angel." Her songs on David's iPod were the ones that hadn't made any sense to me, but suddenly they did. Then they launched into "Ave Maria," a surprisingly Catholic choice, though certainly more predictable for a religious funereal setting than the other music. It had the same effect it always does: the slow, mournful way the notes rose and fell provoking tears.

Tommy took Christopher's little hand and, together, they walked up the few wooden stairs to the pulpit. My brother cried openly standing on the altar while he talked, the mini version of himself close beside him. Tommy's willingness to let his pain show at last, and in such a public way, made me proud of him, but it scared me a little too. I had never seen him emotional in this way.

What I remember most was his simple opening: "Dave was my big brother." At some point, he referenced tow-headed Christopher, his equally red-faced son, as the only other cyclist in the family. His face barely showing above the tall pulpit, Christopher thrust aloft a gold medal attached to a wide ribbon for all to see, a biking award from a race he competed in with David.

When I went back up, I said into the mic emphatically, ever the baby sister trying to prove herself, "David was my big brother too." It was, perhaps, the most important thing I had to say.

As I looked up, I noticed that every row of wooden pews was packed. The back of the church was jammed with people standing two and three deep. The side aisles even had mourners lingering in them. In retrospect, it was one giant fire hazard. In the moment, I was simply in awe. Flashes of orange on wrists marked us all as being part of the same team. I glanced over at the orange bike, realizing that the whole place was color-coordinated. I knew my brother had touched a lot of people and was well loved, but I genuinely had no idea how vast his reach had been. Afterward, someone said they thought there had been at least six hundred attendees, and that number didn't figure in the many who intended to come from out of town but were unable because of travel problems after the hurricane. I don't know where we would have put them. I surely loved him, but I had no idea until that day just how many others did too.

I told the congregation about the formative times when David had babysat me and about the "Humpy and Bumpy" stories, about him teaching me to ride my bike and going on family ski vacations, about how good he made me feel. I wrapped up by remembering one of our last conversations during which I told him that I had fallen in love with another dog and wanted to adopt her but was concerned that my friends were beginning to think I was crazy for having the number of pets we did. Peyton and I already had a dog and four cats; adding to it would create a veritable zoo. My volunteer work at a local humane society could always be a problem. But our family had grown up with eight cats, a dog, and a variety of fish, turtles, and rodents; I only knew how to envision a home full of animals. David repeated his short and sweet, often-delivered, and always-helpful line, "Who cares what anyone else thinks?"

The head of David's radiology practice followed me, reminding us of all the excellent work my brother had done over the past sixteen years. Shaun and Patti introduced the bike. They explained where David had hidden it behind a boulder after he rode up to the base of Blanca Peak, his first to climb that final day and how it had been stolen, yet here it was, already retrieved and brought back to Houston. Each of them told stories of their adventures together. Through the sound system, another song by Alter Bridge and one by Nickelback played, both under the heading "Music for Hiking" in the folded paper program. It was wild in a church setting, the strangest music to soberly sit through, but so perfect for David.

It was, in the end, an entirely unorthodox service, and because of that, appropriate in every way. There were no formal prayers or hymns. There was no cross in the church. No classical music other than "Ave Maria" was played, no choir sang. Unitarians, I learned that day, were a refreshingly laid back and open-minded kind of Christian.

In the parish hall afterward, competing photographic exhibitions of David were on display. Turned out we weren't the only curators of our memories. Mom's corkboard, so carefully designed and organized by hand, with original printed pictures from our lives, looked diminutive and plain set on a table while, across the room, a slideshow was projected onto a large screen with hundreds of images scrolling by in which neither of us was featured. Around the room hung a dozen or so of Glenn's adventure shots, 11x17s printed in dramatic black and white.

When I visited with guests, I fielded the same question over and over: "So, did you get the dog?" Though I had thought the answer was evident in my speech, I had apparently left them all hanging. With a smile, I told each one, "Her name is Trixie."

In preparation for the less-formal celebration of David's life, planned for that night at his house, all I needed was to buy a good bottle of Scotch. His teammates had planned an evening of storytelling and toasts, maybe with pizza. This was my kind of party, though not my mother's, whom I made the mistake of riding with and therefore had to leave with, much earlier than I would have liked.

I had just enough time for lots of hugs from my brother's tremendous friends and a couple of glasses of Scotch with Cheryl. She took a few pictures with her digital camera, and after reviewing one, grabbed my arm. "Look! Right there. Do you see that?"

A bright flash hovered in the corner of the frame. "Oh, yeah. What is that?"

"It looks like a hand! I think it's David. Do you think he's here?" She started showing the photo to others, exclaiming. Who was I to deny signs anyone was seeing? I wondered if we would ever stop looking for him.

Flailing and Centering

Almost immediately after I returned home from David's memorial, I began doubting whether I wanted to continue working at the credit union where I had been marketing manager for two years. It was a great job with truly nice people, and they had shown extreme patience with my extended bereavement leave, but finance wasn't really my thing. I didn't want to spend what I now knew could be a short life promoting used car loans.

I suddenly accepted every invitation to go out with friends—for dinner, music, art shows, book readings, anything, even if it was quite inconvenient—worried I might miss something. I went back to New York City alone on a work night to see Echo and the Bunnymen, a band I'd wanted to see all my life, at Radio City Music Hall, with Peyton's friends (he was *still* on tour). I was so giddy with my ability to seize the day, I even called my mother from the train, as if to gloat, since I knew I was doing something she would probably disapprove of. I was back at work the next morning, bleary-eyed and sleep deprived, but so pleased with myself.

In the months immediately following David's death, I had a new remarkable lack of fear, coupled with a great urgency. I started telling people I was forming a new band even though I hadn't played in one for nearly a decade. I even had all the players picked out and they kindly committed. Also, I needed to write my brother's biography as soon as possible. *He must be memorialized on the page!* And travel. I needed to see the world! I was frantic with this new, clear, painful understanding that someone can die at forty-seven, be snuffed out overnight. There was so much to be done, so much to experience. For months, I repeated to myself, like a personal mantra, *you can sleep when you're dead.*

During that winter, after the wave of cards and phone calls and flowers stopped, after people stopped asking how I was and being willing to talk, after I was supposed to be able to get back to "normal" life, I found myself lonelier than I'd ever been. Friends weren't cruel enough to admit that they were tired of having a grieving friend, but it was clear that some of them would rather I stop dwelling. They stopped asking how I was and changed the subject when I brought up my brother in conversation. Peyton had grown weary. He thought the "shrine" of photos and mementos should be shrinking rather than expanding.

I called my former therapist; I needed to come back. I saw her for a few weeks during which she assured me everything I was feeling was normal. But this normal didn't feel good. I needed something else, something more.

A friend recommended a bereavement writing group that she had once attended after a major loss. It was facilitated by a chaplain at the local hospital. I was so actively, angrily anti-God, this concerned me. Would it be religious? Becky was sensitive and kind and never mentioned anything spiritual as we emailed each other to work out logistics. More than anything, I liked the idea of writing again. I had missed it since abandoning my poetry practice just after college and thought it might help me heal. She invited me to join her next ten-week session and I accepted.

I was all nerves that first Tuesday night as I entered the meeting-house of the local retirement community where her groups met. When I tentatively called out to what seemed an empty building, "Hello?" a friendly face peered around the corner. The good news about hospital chaplains in Northampton, Massachusetts, is that they are more like divine hippies than priests. Or at least Becky is. With her flowing pants and sandals, short-cropped gray hair, silver jewelry, and warm smile, she was utterly disarming.

Eight of us gathered in the tiny library of the meetinghouse, seated around a table, facing each other, surrounded by shelves of books on all sides, which comforted me. Each of us wore a "Hello my name is" sticky tag with our first names scrawled across them in black marker. Becky lit a tea light that was placed in the middle of the tables. "This is in memory and in honor of those who brought us there," she said softly. She asked us to close our eyes and arrive in the moment. "Like a boat that comes to a stop in a pond. Think about the ripples it makes as it stills."

This was as spiritual as it would get, and the small meditation became a therapeutic centering activity for me each week as I left behind the noise of the rest of my daily life and came to rest there among unlikely friends, buoyed as if floating on water. My whole body sighed.

After these openings, Becky would give us writing prompts, often something simple like, "Think of a photograph and then start by writing 'In this one...' and keep going" or "Write 'Tonight what's on my mind is...' and follow that thought without stopping."

I call it looking into the fire, what we're doing here, I wrote.

The world makes it impossible to carve out the time, the focus, the energy to look. It actively encourages us to avert our eyes. Being a mess is not socially acceptable. Calling out from work because of heartache is frowned upon, not that I've dared to try. But stuffing it down inside is like tamping gunpowder, knowing a discharge, an explosion, is inevitable.

We go between "real" life—faker than fake so we don't upset anyone— and looking into this fire. Despite the eye-hurting brightness in the darkness, the heat, the danger in looking. There is bigger danger in never looking. In looking away.

It's like the way candles can light each other's wicks without losing any of their own energy, passing the flame on. The way an ember can fly and ignite a forest. The fear is seeing it all rage out of control. But averting our eyes is like waiting for a sudden backdraft.

Is it some kind of masochism, revisiting the pain, letting it burn me again? Or is it the overwhelming need to etch my memories, like a brand, onto myself?

There is a discipline to it, learning how to toast a marshmallow instead of burning down an entire house. Figuring out the hole inside of us instead of ignoring it and listening to it tick like a bomb.

Consider the controlled burn or the intentional fires set to offset other ones. Cleaning out the pine needles, dry leaves, the kindling of our hearts to avoid self-immolation later.

Imagine keeping this fire lit, rather than letting it turn to ashes or watering it into a sopping mess. It requires stoking. It requires attention and care. It needs oxygen. Look into the fire appreciating how full of energy it is, with potential for destruction or to shed a vital light.

Sometimes Becky's prompts involved the reading of a poem, choosing picture postcards, or selecting a trinket from one of her many boxes of treasures and letting it provoke something. We would free-write for ten or twenty minutes, during which

112

all you could hear was the soft scratching of pens on paper or the clicking of laptop keys, an inhale or sigh, a grab for a tissue. After Becky quietly told us it was time to wrap it up, we would go around the table one by one and read to each other the fresh, raw things we had written. Whatever poured out of us each time was okay, even if the writing basically sucked. There were strict rules for responding, enforced gently. Group members could only focus on what they liked in the writing and had to refer to the "narrator" or "writer" instead of addressing anyone directly as "you." This arms-length distance was intended to protect us from any insult or offense given the intimacy and vulnerability of our material. Sobs and long pauses were frequent. Though most of us made it through without breaking down, some readers couldn't go on. This, too, was okay.

Unlike everywhere else in my life, this was a space where everyone was broken. Everyone was bereft. Everyone was trying to feel better. Not "get over it," but figure out a way to live with the new holes in our lives by writing them out on the page. Whether they had lost a husband, mother, son, or brother, these people got it in a way no one else did. We were all a mess, and we needed a place where our messiness didn't bother anyone else. And in that misery-loves-company way, we became deeply bonded over our mutual grief. We quickly became comfortable showing the naked, terrible, sorrowful, ugly, and damaged parts of ourselves on paper and saying these things out loud. I was always exhausted, but relieved, and terribly glad I had come.

I loved being among other "losers" and writing through my pain, participating in four sessions over four years. It felt self-indulgent in a way, yet I decided I deserved it. The fact that I had found a place to immerse myself in my grief rather than shy away from it solved the problem I had in the outside world, where everyone else had moved on and assumed I had too. At writing group, no one acted like I shouldn't need to be there anymore, like something was wrong with me because I needed to keep processing. People who were five or seven or ten years out from their initial losses had come to this library in order to stop feeling like freaks.

Every week during the first session, as I drove home with the stories of the group swirling in my head, I wondered whether I could properly explain that sanctuary, and its importance, to Peyton. At the time, I was spinning Neko Case's new album *Middle Cyclone* on repeat every time I got in my car. I listened as I drove through late winter snow, processing the evening's readings, attempting to distill my sense of anguish and consolation into something he would relate to, her words about tornados and last rites and vengeance pounding through my brain.

I so wanted to connect with Peyton over my experience of loss and wondered why it was so hard. He had experienced the early death of lots of friends; so many, in fact, he told me he could have covered both of his arms with tattoos of their names. There had been overdoses, accidents, suicides, cancer. Had he just become immune? Was it all too painful to face? Did he want desperately to focus on something—anything—else? I wished it was something I could share with him, and that he could understand me, the me I had become, this way.

Each group—just like people and the many ways we grieve, or don't—was different. Personalities matched beautifully or didn't quite. Some people were reliable about attending each week; others just couldn't handle it after a while. Some people talked too much, others not enough. But we patiently put up with each other because, after all, it was the only place we were all accepted as our whole broken selves. Where everyone "got it." My third group clicked particularly well—we had a little reunion a few months after the formal session had ended, and I have stayed friends with two of the participants. We check in with each other occasionally about how our grieving is progressing.

Knowing it will never be done.

So Many Questions, Most of Them Wrong

Other oft-asked questions in response to hearing the news that David had died included, "Was he married?" and "Did he have kids?" These were delivered sometimes in lieu of, but surprisingly often, in tandem with, "Were you close?"

Because the answers to these two questions were simple and factual, they were easier to spit out, "No" and "No." But the internal processing was complicated. My gut reaction was always, *why are you asking that? Does it matter?* And then, angrily, feeling entirely invisible, *oh, you're worried about some unknown wife and children instead of the person you know who is standing here. Isn't that kind of you.* Also, *Cheryl is devastated, if you must know, but because they weren't legal—she was only a girlfriend—I guess she doesn't count.*

I know now that people are trying to demonstrate interest with good intention, and that these are the generic questions society has deemed acceptable to ask of people you don't know, but they aren't usually helpful and can often be extremely unhelpful. (I have a friend who, after several miscarriages, three rounds of IVF, and a baby who died after being born prematurely, might punch you in the face if you asked her whether she had kids, depending on what kind of day she was having.) It would have been so much better if instead people had thought to simply say, "Tell me about him." Or, "What did David do? What did he like?" if they wanted to chat about it.

A long-time friend had flowers delivered to my office shortly after I returned home from Houston. The cheery colorful bouquet sat at the edge of my desk nearly begging for inquiry, which I was feeling ambiguous about. So, I was damn near ecstatic when a coworker, learning about my loss simply replied, "I'm so sorry to hear that. Please let me know if I can help you with anything," and left it at that. Sympathy and no questions.

Even though I would shut down inquirers with definitive answers in the negative—that David wasn't married and didn't have children—and assume our conversation was over, some felt the need to keep questioning me, though even then most people still didn't ask me how I was feeling. Instead, they would follow up with something like, "How are your parents?"

All I ever wanted to say was, *they're a mess! Wouldn't you be? But they aren't here. I'm right here in front of you, and I'm hurting so much.* Instead, I did what we have been trained to do, delivering some bullshit so as to keep things light in the face of such heaviness. "Yeah, it's pretty tough for them as you can imagine, but they're keeping it together."

I understand that a plain, "How are you?" under the circumstances might sound absurd. The assumption that a person isn't going to be feeling good when they've just lost someone is certainly a fair one, but it's really one of the best questions—especially for those who can handle a real answer. I can't count how many times perfectly nice people wouldn't even mutter, "How are you holding up?" which would have provoked a simpler response and still felt truly kind. Instead, they'd distance themselves even further, making obvious declarative statements like, "Your poor mom."

Yes, my poor mom. It's not as though I ever thought for a minute that she didn't deserve pity—she absolutely did, and does. *But hellooooooooo. Look at me!*

No one knows what to say. It's not their fault. We, as a culture, are so inept at talking about death and dying, loss and grief. Worrying over how to address a bereaved person can paralyze us with fear, so we avoid it at all costs. We wither with discomfort and shrink away just when the bereaved need us most. We shudder even writing a sympathy card. Most of us are uneasy acknowledging that death is part of life, though losses are the only experiences guaranteed to happen to all of us at some point. We don't want to make an utterance that could touch a nerve or make someone break down because we would be even more unequipped to handle that, because we don't talk about this stuff. It's a vicious cycle.

Dealing with sibling deaths, I learned, was even more fraught. Stories on coping with the death of a parent, spouse, or child are ever-present. After scouring the shelves at my local bookstore and searching online, I was shocked to only find two books that addressed the extremely common, yet largely overlooked experience of losing a brother or sister—*The Empty Room* by Elizabeth DeVita-Raeburn and *Surviving the Death of a Sibling* by T. J. Wray. Both writers are women whose brothers died. The dearth of material on the subject told me as much about it as what the pages in the books did, but I was grateful to have found what I did, especially with these relatable relationships.

Both reference the term *disenfranchised grief*, coined by counselor, author, and grief expert, Kenneth Doka. Defined as a loss that is not publicly acknowledged or as widely accepted as others, disenfranchised grief finally considers the "forgotten mourners," those who feel inadequately respected or consoled by their communities because their loss doesn't fit into a prescribed idea of which deaths really matter: same-sex or trans partners, miscarriages and abortions, friends, pets, and even nuclear family relations: siblings. New to me, the phrase *disenfranchised grief* validated my feelings of being overlooked or entirely unseen.

Wray writes, "...within days of my brother's death, I learned an important lesson. I learned that no matter how paralyzed with grief and sorrow I might have felt, society does not recognize the death of an adult brother or sister as a *major loss*." I had felt so similarly unentitled in the aftermath of David's death.

In the forward of Wray's book, published in 2003, Professor Emeritus of Pastoral Psychology and Family Studies J. Earl Thompson opens, "It's amazing that after more than fifty years of reflection upon the psychology of bereavement, there has been almost no attention to adult sibling loss."

Though eighty percent of Americans have at least one brother or sister, the majority of whom will die in adulthood, most of us end up sensing we are alone in our suffering or that we are mourning improperly—for too long, with too much emotion. That the consideration truly should be given to others higher up on the "hierarchy of grief." Sibling research only began in earnest in the 1980s; generations of psychotherapists and "grief experts" overlooked it. There is still much to try to understand.

The predictable and annoying inquiries about marriage and kids and parents are the kind said in order to say *something*. They are borne out of pure apprehension and an urge not to stay silent, which is often worse. And I'm entirely certain that, before my experience of grief changed my perspective forever, I asked them too. But I've never felt as alienated as I did when people inquired this way, over and over, as if I were representing my family and not an actual part of it.

"The very nature of disenfranchised grief creates additional problems for grief, while removing or minimizing sources of support," wrote Doka in his book on the subject.

If I had been able to respond in the affirmative that David was married or had kids, I am confident that the focus would then have been how terrible it must be for them, just like how terrible it must be for our mom or his dad, and not how terrible it was for Tommy or for me—or for the other half- and step-brothers and sisters, which number several more—as David's siblings. Why, I wondered, did no one act as though we were just as injured by this experience?

It was inconceivable to me that anyone who discovered that Mom had lost a son then asked her, "Did he have brothers or sisters?" We have at least all been taught how unnatural, how sad, and how fundamentally wrong it is for a child to predecease a parent, how that is the wrong natural order of things, how painful it must be to say goodbye to a person that sprang from one's own womb, that this is, socially, the pinnacle of the hierarchy of grief.

But our siblings are the people we know, typically, our whole lives. They come of age with us, they survive marriages, dislocation, job woes, babies, and divorces with us, and long after our parents are gone, we expect they will grow old with us.

"While all families are unique and different (we all have our secrets, crazy relatives, embarrassing stories, and wonderful, magical moments), only your brothers and sisters know first-hand what it was like to grow up in your particular family," Wray writes. "Losing a sibling, then, can also mean losing a part of yourself, part of that special connection to the past. How do we learn to live with the broken circle that is now our family?"

When I first told Tommy I was writing about David, I asked him, "So, when your friends and coworkers found out, did they all first ask if he was married?"

"Yes!" he said immediately, seeming surprised.

"And then they asked whether there were kids?"

"Yes!"

"Did you get grilled about how Mom was?" I continued.

He answered affirmatively for a third time. "How did you know?"

Lastly, "Did you feel like you didn't matter? Like somehow they didn't even think about the fact that you were devastated too?"

"Yes!" Tommy replied and started to cry.

I began to feel in that moment that it wasn't true that the only thing Tommy and I had in common was our love of David. There was the painful fact that we both spent years feeling alone and unentitled to our sense of loss. Though I would never have wished for him to feel the same pain and isolation, I was intensely grateful for the connection. That day, I was reminded that we are bonded in ways I'll never be bonded to anyone else in the world. And I knew I had his blessing to write this book.

Icarus

On a cold December night a few months after David died, I went to a local tattoo parlor and had a flying bird permanently emblazoned on the back of my right shoulder. I had been thinking about the mythological character Icarus in relationship to David, and I wanted to do something memorial. A bird seemed vaguely spiritual, and, dwelling on the question of how my brother had had such an accident, my mind had been spinning around the concept of flying too close to the sun.

I already had a large sun tattooed on the back of my left shoulder. I planned to have the artist place the bird on the opposite shoulder, at the same level as the sun, flying toward it, but not anywhere close to it—my way of affixing him a safe distance from danger, if also facing it.

The bird I selected was a swallow, feathered wings raised high, beak slightly open. Swallows were classic tattoos of sailors, received after traveling their first five thousand nautical miles. The experience of surviving David's death felt like such a rite of passage, as though I had traveled a similarly great distance in my life at that point, symbolically anyway, whatever that meant. Legend also suggested that, because real swallows return to the same spot each year to mate, sailors bearing these tattoos would return from their journeys safely—if David hadn't, maybe I could assure that I would? A third bit of lore mentioned that if a swallow-tattooed sailor drowned, the swallow would carry his soul to heaven.

I was ascribing meaning all over the place.

I asked the artist to color the swallow with some pops of orange in honor of David's last bike, the one that had been a stand-in for a coffin at his funeral, and the memorial bracelet that I was still wearing. I didn't mention this meaning to Ben, a lumbering guy who listened to indie rock while his needle buzzed away behind my right ear and while I fixed my stare into the corner of his booth, trying to stay as still as possible. I didn't want to talk about my dead brother with a stranger, not even the one who was making permanent marks on my flesh, not even considering how many people get memorial tattoos. I was afraid my story would either provoke another question I didn't need, or make him sad.

Thinking of David like Icarus, considering that maybe on the fourteeners that day, he had behaved with similar overconfidence, made me furious. I tried to reframe the myth in my head while wincing at the raw scratching on my shoulder: Perhaps David was just so high on the experience and wanted to keep going, that he lacked the ability to stop himself before it was too late. That he soared too high, not from arrogance, but from sheer enjoyment. David lived for achieving feats in the wilderness and likely wondered when he would get back to Colorado to conquer more peaks, to finish his mission of bagging them all. He wasn't the first and won't be the last climber to push himself too far—it happens all the time.

David wasn't foolish or naïve the way Icarus was. Peyton reminded me of his extreme competence and responsible planning for every excursion, and David's teammates affirmed this to me. Altitude might have adversely affected him, of course. Living in Houston means living at sea level. The small city of Alamosa, close to the base of David's last three conquests, sits over 7,500 feet high, already a massive elevation shift for anyone, and that number nearly doubles standing on top of Little Bear Peak.

Icarus was giddy being up so high, and his giddiness made him act like a drunk. Altitude causes a significant decrease in oxygen in the blood, altering one's sense of reality—but David would have been well aware of this as a doctor, scientist, and athlete. Pain, even slight, changes people's perceptions too. I was aware of a slight light-headedness, not all bad, while the drawing was etched onto me.

Had David become too enchanted with spectacular views like the mythological figure I was imagining? Overly ambitious to reach his goal? Psychologists actually use the term "Icarus complex" to describe those who are drawn to both literal heights and positions of power, men mesmerized by fire, seeking admiration, succumbing to *ascensionism*—defined by Wikipedia as "the notion that the future is not dictated by the past or present, and no destination or goal is unreachable *combined with an anticipation of falling.*"

Could my brother ever have anticipated such a moment? Was this part of the thrill? Even a motivating force somehow?

I did the only thing I could think of, in ink if not in life, to keep my brother safe, keep him with me, keep him aloft, keep him alive. A stop-motion flight, a still frame of his journey, my brother's spirit flying eternally—or at least for as long as I am here.

Impact

Despite the outlet the writing group provided, outside of it, I often didn't know what to do with my own mind, which refused to stop chewing on my loss. Plus, I didn't want any part in the distractions others seemed to think would be helpful. I didn't want to stop thinking about my brother at all, for fear that I would forget the sound of his voice or the way his eyes crinkled at the edges when he smiled, or the easy way he had about him, so comfortable in his own skin. I had become so uncomfortable in mine.

One day at work, the year after his death, I Googled his name. I wasn't sure what I was looking for but was eager to find something, anything, to feel less alone. "David Boyd" isn't a one-of-a-kind name, so I anticipated having to do some digging. Maybe I'd need to search with his middle name, as well, and look under "Dave," the nickname I never used but which Tommy and all his friends did. Maybe I'd add keywords like "MOAT," "Primal Quest," "adventure racing," or the name of his radiological practice.

None of this was needed.

Not only were the results on the first page all about my particular David Boyd, so were the second and third and fourth and fifth, and so on. With few exceptions, every search result was about him. My eyes widened as I scrolled.

There were news articles with headlines like, "Another Climbing Death" and "Man with SPOT Dies on Little Bear," referring to the GPS locator he had with him. David and his team also showed up in several leaderboards on racing sites. Many pictures of him dressed in bright athletic garb in outside settings surfaced.

The Texas Mountain Bike Racing Association's "Rider Board" had a discussion thread that had been started within two days of the news of his accident. There were dozens of posts, starting with both friends and strangers discussing the mystery.

Someone with the handle 10E started: "Some close friends and family members gathered this morning to come to an under-standing of what might have happened on Little Bear Peak. We know this: Dave left the RV at 0625 Wednesday en route to the summits of Blanca Peak, Ellingwood Peak, and Little Bear Peak … he reached the base of Little Bear at 1310 … gained the top of the ridge at 1332 … descended the hourglass at 1508 … and the next SPOT transmission did not go out until 2118 that evening, 200 feet below the ridgeline."

The precise military time was startling, as it sounded like it was straight from a device, like the SPOT beacon mentioned, and I wondered where those details had come from. As I read, I got distracted trying to translate to standard time in order to follow along.

10E continued: "Stories of Dave being stranded atop the moun-tain waiting in vain for help to appear did not end up being true. Dave did not get cliffed out nor did he get lost in the dark. He did not reach a state of exhaustion to where he could not continue. This was the fortieth 14,000-foot Colorado mountain that Dave had climbed. Bagging doubles and triples was commonplace. Add that to all the 100-milers, Primal Quests, and multi-day adventure races and you can tell he was experienced with the great outdoors. Word from one of the SAR respondents was that Dave was one of the most well-prepared hikers they had come across. His pack was filled with spare clothes, medical supplies, SPOT beacon, Garmin GPS, and, of course, duct tape."

Who was this 10E and how did he/she/they know so much, so much that I didn't know? What did it mean to "get cliffed out"? What were these 100-milers? I didn't know what a SPOT beacon was before this happened. I had never heard of a four-teener before this happened. There was so much new nomenclature to learn.

10E finished his/her/their post about David's last hike with this: "He was prepared for everything except what we cannot control." I shuddered. Still, I read on. The conversation shifted, to my relief. Someone named Doug talked about making memorial bracelets to wear at races in David's honor. *Ah, this is where the inspiration came from,* I thought.

A Cynthia S. wrote: "As a joke, about a year ago, someone did make WWDBD bracelets, as he was the tuff guy that could tackle anything. Now the bracelet has taken on more meaning than a smack joke."

Finally, I recognized the name Wink, who chimed in, "If someone could get me a WWDBD wristband, I would be willing to pay it."

On and on it went as dozens of people talked about this original wristband, who made it, whether they should make more, if the bracelets should be sold to raise money for biking causes, whether they should read the same way as the first batch, what sizes should be made, who would pay for them. Everyone wanted one.

I cried as I read, grateful for these incredible notes, but also feeling a bit like a spy, as if I had intruded on a secret club of people I mostly didn't know, all of whom were bereft but, just like my brother, ready to act, ready to do something meaningful instead of sit around.

Finally, Kim Chance, a name I recognized as one of David's bicycling friends, said, "The team would like to encourage the production of the WWDBD bracelets. In fact, if we could get 500-1000 of them by this Friday ... Shaun suggested making them in the color orange ... The same color as Dave's last bike."

I now had the story about what had transpired to fill the church with orange cuffs at David's memorial. But I had much more to learn about how dramatically his life affected so many others and what a big part of the Texas biking community he was, what a presence he had been, such a leader. The stories proved, just as the sight of people crammed into the church at the memorial had, that my big brother meant just as much to many other people as he did to Tommy and me. I read more, fascinated and touched by the outpouring of grief, admiration, and shock as well as the desire to recognize him: "I can attest to how super Dave was. He was encouraging and inspiring and always asking what he could do to make things happen and to get others involved. He truly personified the life of a great outdoorsman and was a class act."

Some even reflected on how his early death inspired them to do more: "...we only have so much time here, so we better make the most of every minute just like Dave."

Days later, I again indulged myself by locating additional posts on 14ers.com in a thread in memory of my brother. Not only had David become a bit of a legend in Texas and had been chipping away at his new climbing goal without my knowledge, but he had also joined a large alliance of climbers who were all interested in this famous group of mountains. And *everyone* was talking about him.

I read seventy-five posts, imagining that they would all be kind remembrances, but many more contributors went back and forth speculating about what might have happened: could it have snowed, was there hail or rain, did David stumble on a loose rock? It both hurt and consoled me to realize others had been so tormented. They discussed misinformation from various news reports: some printed that he had sent emergency signals for hours. Papers suggested that he was in an altogether different part of the Sangre de Cristo mountain range. One article described "his wife" calling search and rescue.

The climbers talked about having been in some of the same places, starting at Lake Como, just beneath Little Bear. Eerily, a number of people had seen my brother on his final hike, including a group of four guys who posted the picture David took of them when they met on Blanca Peak, his first of three that last day. "We had just summited when Dr. Boyd came dashing up behind us in his bright red running shoes ..." a man named Scott wrote. "He stayed and chatted with us for a few minutes, then dashed off as quickly as he came, and began his attack on the Blanca-Ellingwood Ridge. The last time I remember seeing him was when he climbed too high at one point and had to down-climb and try again. Our group was barely past the low point in the ridge when he reached the Ellingwood summit. I was so impressed with him that I made a point to look up his name on the Ellingwood register when I got there."

His friend Paul added, "At approx. 3pm. that day we went to Lake Como to pack up our gear and hike out. At that time, we heard an incredibly loud rock slide and could clearly see the dust rising everywhere in the area."

Scott responded: "As Paul mentions above, our group heard what must certainly have been the rock slide precipitated by his fall...Was the rock slide in the vicinity of the access gully for Little Bear?"

Then people in more than a few posts reported wanting to traverse the same peaks right after David, attempting to understand more, seeing if they could pick up the registers—the books at the tops of mountains where climbers sign their names to prove they made it. I hadn't even known such records existed. One guy wrote, "I can juggle my plans and head down there ... I'm not the peak gladiator Dave was, but I'll do what I can."

I was so grateful for their insistence and courage—above all, for their equal need to know. They were going where I wanted to but couldn't. They even posted pictures of the lake and surrounding areas, as if, at least in my magical thinking, they knew I wanted to see what they were talking about. Lake Como at sunset appeared serene as the water on the surface mirrored the soft pink and yellow sky, a thick swath of pine trees near the water with an enormous barren ledge behind it. This was the infamous Little Bear. A shot showed the peak from above, gray-brown and dry, looking utterly plain to me. I could see the sharpness of the rock at the summit, and the view beyond was impressively expansive. I wished I could tell exactly where David had walked, where he had fallen, where he had landed.

People on the discussion boards described the way Hurricane Ike had delayed the memorial service in celestial terms: "The spirits are not happy with this event."

Bike Texas listed a memorial post: "Known and respected by other racers for his athleticism, humility, generosity, and good sportsmanship, his untimely death has inspired an outpouring of grief and remembrance from the mountain bike and climbing communities."

Adventure World Magazine ran an entire "Remembering Dave Boyd" article, where they outlined the many accomplishments my brother had been too humble to announce to all of us: "Dave won two adventure race state championships, three mountain bike state championships, two cyclocross state championships, five adventure race national championships, the TransRockies Race Series, and double gold buckles at the Leadville Trail 100."

When I read these impressive reports, I felt like I was reading about someone else. When asked how races went, David had always focused on how much fun he had. I heard about the landscapes he saw, the people he met, the challenging sections. A friend said one of their favorite things about David was that when they raced, it wasn't all about the race. They went on side trips hiking to see beautiful views or practice rappelling off bridges or to ride down country roads. I almost never heard about wins.

The double buckles from Leadville are now hung on our mom's dining room wall. I had to read the newspaper article from the *Houston Chronicle* that is framed with them to understand their significance. As it happens, it's quite something to win. "The Leadville 100 is one of the most revered mountain-bike challenges on the planet," it read. "It is also one of the toughest 100-mile ultramarathons. Dave Boyd thought this was a good year to give them both a shot." To earn these buckles, competitors have to finish the mountain bike race in less than nine hours and the running component in under twenty-five, both within seven days of each other.

Good god, he did that? I thought. There was so much I hadn't heard about.

His teammates and friends shared more profound "Dr. Dave memories": he often gave his racing prizes away to other competitors; he not only paid for a teammate's plane ticket to a competition, but also for her son and his friend to attend; he dealt with alligators while trying to find a checkpoint in a race; he laughed when literally stuck between a rock and a hard place while climbing with a friend. Someone wrote about my brother essentially saving him from hypothermia during a paddling event, which he went on to win, and then gave the guy the wristwatch he had been awarded. They called him "Super Dave," "the silent giver," "the ultimate competitor," "super human," "a true super hero," "a master." Proud as I was, it was kind of refreshing when I got to the simplicity of Shaun recalling how, when competing, what David wanted for food was so simple: "sandwiches and bars. That's how we roll."

Cheryl had logged a long note to everyone on the fourteeners board: "I know how special this group is to Dave, and I wanted to share ..." *She* knew. I didn't know. Where had I been? "He spent every day before his death climbing, hiking, and riding," she wrote. "And he flew me, my daughter, Aubrey, and his nephew, Christopher, to Denver for their first camping trip. The night before his death, he called his brother and had a forty-five-minute conversation. The lesson I learned from Dave is never to take your life for granted."

Though I was both happy and envious knowing Tommy and Cheryl had those last calls, I wished I had had one. My final chat with my brother had taken place weeks before that. I hadn't asked about his next trip, and I missed out on so much. I wanted the opportunity to turn back time and learn so much more.

The circle of friends and well-wishers was growing incrementally by the minute, outwardly larger and larger, like a ripple on a lake. By now, their words were practically drowning me, yet I kept going. "We all know the risk we take going into the mountains," another climber wrote, "but it's still painful when we get the news that another of us is gone." I discovered how many of the remembrances were written by strangers, people who maybe knew *about* him before his death, but also many who never met him, but who said, "from all of the posts here, I wish that I had."

Fear of Falling

Early in our relationship, Peyton had invited me to go hiking with him on Norwottuck, the mountain closest to our college campus. I wasn't well practiced or even terribly interested in hiking, but, newly in love, I was keen to do things he enjoyed, and this was one of those things. I did passably on short stretches, but whined on the long ones. Still, we hiked there and beyond.

After dating a couple of years, we went to his aunt and uncle's cabin in New Hampshire just off of Squam Lake on the southern edge of the White Mountains. Hiking there was more intense than the trails in western Massachusetts, most of which topped out at only a thousand or so feet. But the payoff was also greater when we were willing to go more like four thousand feet: high views of the open sky through the silhouettes of evergreens overlooked the enormous sparkling lake dotted with tiny islands and even tinier boats throwing pencil-thin white wakes. It gave me a new appreciation for what summiting even minor mountains could do.

Peyton took me up the Rattlesnakes, a pair of low peaks overlooking Squam, where we stopped at the top to perch on enormous granite boulders hanging over the lake, share a beer and an apple, and drink in the view. He guided me to the top of Red Hill to its defunct fire tower. I climbed the series of rickety stairs without hesitation and saw the hills unfold in the distance in all directions.

"You can see four states from here!" he told me, pointing out various mountain ranges, the green sides of which softly blurred to pale blues and purples in the distance. "There's Vermont." He pointed toward what I trusted was west of us, having inherited none of the geographic sensibility of my brother. "And there's Maine, New Hampshire, and home, Massachusetts," Peyton showed me, excitedly marching around the tower counterclockwise.

Another favored spot was Eagle Cliff, which boasted a white rocky face so large, we could see across the lake from the deck of the cabin more than a mile away. It became a "must-do" hike each time we visited, and it was a joy to experience in spring, summer, and fall, watching the flora change on our path from surprising forest flowers to lush beds of moss to red and gold leaves.

Once we adopted our dogs, Hank and Trixie, they, too, became hikers. And they were as thrilled as Peyton, if not more so, to hit the trails, especially in New Hampshire where we were less likely to encounter other dogs and they were regularly let off-leash. The uncommon freedom was especially easy with Hank, who despite his delight in roaming, was always checking in, regularly stopping ahead of us on the path to turn his head and make sure we were bringing up the rear.

Other hikers we encountered often laughed at Hank, a corgi. "Poor dog!" they would say. "His little legs; he must be so tired."

"He's a far better hiker than we are," we told them each time. "Just watch him go." And Hank would hop up small boulders more easily than the stairs at home, moving with the agility of a deer over logs and roots, clearly eager to go faster, looking back at us as if to communicate, "Come on, you guys! What's the hold up?"

Our trip to New Hampshire during the summer following David's death brought with it equal parts happiness and angst. I had thought of him on many of our annual trips, knowing how much he would love not just the hiking, but also the opportunities to canoe, water ski, and go fishing. This cabin experience, other than the location's greater elevation, had so much in common with the East Texas cabin that had been our family's refuge from the city growing up. The place itself had many of the same and similar features: interiors of natural wood, windows looking out onto dense trees in all directions, a high-ceilinged, open area as the central feature, a woodstove in lieu of a fireplace, a deck instead of a porch. Even walks through the woods reminded me of our childhood get-away, as pine needles underfoot gave off the same earthy perfume, views through the trees showed glints of sunshine bouncing off the lake, plentiful birds filled the air with song. He would have loved it there.

The first priority, as usual, was Eagle Cliff. Our first full day, we packed sandwiches in a backpack, put the dogs in the backseat, and drove the narrow dirt roads down to the main road, where the trailhead started. The beginning of the hike is deeply forested; birch, pine, and maple trees shade the trail and obscure any sights other than the woods themselves. As one meanders upward on the leaf-strewn path, things open up a bit, but it takes until reaching more than halfway to the top to have much of a view. With Hank off-leash as usual, I found myself losing the confidence that I always had with him. At the first lookout, he ran eagerly to the end of a flat rock jutting over the side of the mountain, and immediately my body flushed with nervous adrenaline.

"What's wrong?" Peyton asked as I ran over to clip his leash on and bring him back to the path.

"He's just making me uncomfortable being so close to the edge."

Peyton countered, "He's fine!" After making our way a bit farther, I let Hank off again. Then I fussed over him at another spot where we all had to scramble over a rocky pitch, insisting on not just leashing him up, but also carrying him. But once over that pass, I let him go again.

When we reached the summit, where enormous rocks cap the top of the ridge, preventing tree growth, thus opening it up to the sky and a panoramic vista of the lake, Hank gleefully jogged right over to the lip. Below was a sheer drop of hundreds of feet.

I burst into tears. "He could fall!" I cried as I ran over to him, connected the leash, and pulled him far away from the edge. Clutching my confused dog, I wept as my husband looked on, shock registering in his wide eyes.

"He's not going fall," Peyton said, trying to soothe me. "He's done this dozens of times. He knows what he's doing."

I said, "So did David."

Anything can happen. And, I had learned the hard way, often does. I had never been worried about heights before, never experienced vertigo, never worried about my dog—or my big brother. Knowing what you're doing doesn't necessarily keep you safe.

I had control over so little. If I could protect my beloved dog, this creature that depended on me, even for one minute, even if it made his hike a little less fun, in that moment, I had to. Hank stayed on the leash in my hand the entire way down the trails, which we marched despondently in silence, tears streaming down my cheeks.

The Inversion

A year after David died, I decided to accompany our mom on a trip to the location of his fatal fall. She had been there in the immediate aftermath to take care of the agonizing business of identification. Tommy had made the pilgrimage later, hiring a plane to fly him over the bare, rocky peaks above the tree line. Several of David's teammates had gone back to retrace his steps, finishing the course he had laid out but never completed. I needed to go there too. I needed to face the mountain that killed my brother.

This was the official story we now understood: During the afternoon of September 3, 2008, David summited Little Bear Peak at the southern end of the Sangre de Christo Mountains. He signed the register at the top, *3rd Peak Today! Nice & Dry!* Because of his GPS, we know he arrived at the top at precisely 2:49 p.m. Always one for personal challenge, David apparently thought nothing of knocking off three fourteen-thousand-foot mountains in one day, despite the fact that this feat would take most climbers two or even three days.

Late that night, Cheryl reported him missing, since she hadn't heard from him and he was too reliable for this lapse not to worry her. Two days later, after an exhaustive hunt using his

GPS coordinates as a guide, Alamosa Volunteer Search and Rescue discovered David's body at 12,400 feet in a steep gorge in the mountain under Little Bear's peak. It was far from the normal route.

I had to see this mountain range myself. I still had questions.

My mother and I met in Colorado Springs. I landed an hour ahead of her. As I waited in a comfy armchair in the airport for her flight to arrive from Houston, I felt a strange mixture of dread and anticipation. What would it be like to stand under the mountain, that behemoth? Would I sense David's presence by being so close to where he had last stood? Would the scenery be beautiful enough to justify the risks he took? Would this experience give me the closure I so desperately sought?

I listened to David's iPod as I waited, falling in love with all of the songs on the album *In Your Honor* by the Foo Fighters. The title wasn't lost on me. It felt intimate to wear the earbuds that had last been anchored in his ears. Dust was caught in the clear plastic back of the iPod case, and I couldn't help imagining that these particles had been picked up on the mountains. Could grains like these have been lodged under his fingernails? Were they fragments of shale, limestone, sandstone, or even gabbro—a volcanic rock I'd never heard of before researching the area?

At last, Mom arrived. She hugged me too hard and too long—almost desperately—the way she had come to do in recent months. It made me claustrophobic, but I let her.

We picked up the small SUV that she had rented and drove an hour and a half south on I-25. The weather was cool, but vibrantly sunny, and the landscape was a display of opposites. In mostly shared silence, we surveyed expansive spans of flat, dry brown earth that backed up onto enormous tree-dappled mountains with snowy peaks in the distance. Every edge of the horizon was framed by them. Occasionally, we passed a patch of earth that yielded scrub brush or yellowing grasses swaying in the breeze. I was surprised by how desert-like the land was, since during my former trips to the state, I had been in deeply green, heavily forested regions, among powder-packed trails.

I hadn't been to Colorado since I was fifteen. We were one of those Texan families who spent most of our winter and spring breaks skiing, and I had spent my earliest trips, at four, five, and six years old, on the mountains with David and Tommy. We all loved going to a place so different from home, bundling in exotic long underwear, snow pants, gloves, and goggles, and swishing our way down trails with spectacular vistas.

This part of Colorado looked like what I imagined the Wild West might have looked like. It was pretty in a dusty, rustic, lonely sort of way.

Our ultimate destination was the Blanca Massif Range of the Sangre de Cristos near Alamosa. But Mom had chosen a small hotel in the nearby town of La Veta, which her online research had convinced her would be more charming. This, combined with the list of local attractions she brought with her, was some-what puzzling, given the nature of our trip.

As we turned off the main road, it was just starting to get dark. La Veta, home to a population of only eight hundred, is nestled closely beneath a pair of stately mountains called the Spanish Peaks. The area was already considered off-season when we arrived in early October, and only three restaurants were open, but one was conveniently on the ground floor of our inn, a place with a quaint terracotta facade.

Over enchiladas, Mom and I discussed the sign at the check-in desk regarding watching out for black bears in the area, the quaintness of the town, how scenic the area was, everything but going to the mountain.

"Tomorrow, I think we should just poke around the area, get acclimated with the surroundings," she said, pulling out a travel book.

"Okay, I guess," I said. "Can I get another beer?" I tried to wave down our waitress.

"Well, what would you like to do?"

"I don't know. That's fine," I replied, having arrived with no agenda other than to see The Mountain, and too tired to argue. I resigned myself to allowing her a day or two to get her bearings before I pushed.

It had taken a lot out of me just to agree to go on a trip with my mom. Though we'd grown closer in the year since David's fall, and I wanted to see this place, it wasn't exactly my idea of a vacation. My one demand was that we not have to share a bed, so she had reserved a suite with a bedroom for her adjacent to a little living room with a pullout couch for me. I settled in that night, unable to stop thinking about David and his proximity to this place during his last days.

We woke up the next morning to a harsh gray day. It was suddenly extremely cold, and a leaden sky pressed down. I had encouraged my mother to pack a down coat and she was grateful to have done so. We dressed warmly and headed to the lobby to find they weren't serving breakfast and were pointed in the direction of a building catty-corner from the inn.

As we crossed the quiet street, completely devoid of traffic, we noticed heavy, low fog making visibility difficult and draping the town in somberness. Everything seemed asleep in the muddled light. We could see our breath escape in small clouds as we expressed our surprise at the dramatic shift in weather from the day before.

The building we entered was set up for traveling campers, providing showers and a small store as well as a modest café. The wood paneled dining room was warm, and the place served the basics—eggs, bacon, toast. It would do the job. We stuck out like the interlopers we were among the handful of regulars there, who were discussing the weather, an "inversion," over coffee.

"An inversion?" we interrupted.

"Oh, yeah," a guy in a flannel shirt said. "It gets like this once in a while, though it's rare. Usually, it's warmer close to the ground and cold in the mountains, but now it's the opposite. See, it's colder down low here in the valley and warmer up high—everything is flip-flopped."

"Is it supposed to stay this cold?" Mom shivered. It was only twenty degrees at 10 a.m.

"Who knows? This ice fog could last a while. Probably won't burn off for a long time. If you want to get warmer, you should go higher."

As we trudged back to the inn, we noticed ice crystals had enveloped flowers and grasses, all still colorful, but shocked frozen. Tree branches appeared fuzzy with their coatings of dense white frost. I started the car and headed through town, down the one main street to Highway 12, where we would work our way to higher ground.

For many miles, the fog clung to everything. It blurred our vision, masked trees, and hung over barns oppressively. Barbed wire fences were encrusted with icy shards, making them appear even more jagged and dangerous than they already were. As we felt the road rising, we finally broke through the dense haze and emerged into another world, a sharp blue sky making it as extreme in its brightness as the other world was opposite in its chronic dusk.

We explored the San Isabel National Forest, winding our way along narrow dirt roads with steep overhangs that made my mother edgy and reminded me of my breakdown with Hank in New Hampshire. The mountains were already significantly snowy in October, though a lake we stumbled across was not yet frozen over. We stopped in the tiny town of Cuchara and browsed the gift shop aimlessly, as if trying to kill time.

"Do you think Peyton would like a wolf t-shirt as a souvenir?" Mom asked, semi-joking.

"Ha!" I said, thinking wistfully of my husband whom I had refused to bring on the trip because I thought it was important to do this with Mom. Now I missed him a lot. "Maybe a worry-rock with a wolf etched into it," I suggested instead, fingering a display of highly polished multi-colored stones emblazoned with a variety of spirit animals.

We talked at length with the proprietor about the inversion, who confirmed it was a somewhat rare and odd phenomenon. Strolling the short streets, I admired their old authentic totem pole and humble log cabins, soaking up the sunshine in the elevation of the town.

Before dark, we headed back to La Veta. As we got closer and the road began to descend, swirling banks of profuse mist ahead of us swallowed the mountains, and our moods sunk with it. It looked as though the pavement was funneling us toward some underworld, enveloped in fog. Instead of burning off as we assumed it would, the unnerving weather from the morning had evidently stalled, keeping the town shrouded in icy gray all day. Mom and I were reverently quiet.

Grateful for sunshine even in lower altitudes the following day, we decided to drive far south, way below our real destination, and I began to wonder if we were, at this point, consciously avoiding it. We meandered through several dry, flyspeck towns admiring wall murals painted in deep earthy burgundies and greens on the baked-brown sides of adobe buildings and exploring Colorado's oldest church, in Conejos, replete with impressive double bell towers and an ancient-looking graveyard with simple wooden crosses laid out in neat rows. Momentarily, I reflected with sadness on the fact that David had no grave to visit. We stopped in Mosca at its one and only store, and seemingly its only building, for a soda, then meandered slowly along the Rio Grande where the landscape was as pure and unadulterated as I'd ever seen. No homes, cars, or buildings of any kind. Not even an electrical power line could be seen for miles.

"Maybe we could drive by the mountain when we get back to the area?" I asked Mom. She easily talked me into Mexican food for dinner in a nearby town instead, after which we turned in early.

On the third day of our four-day weekend, we rambled around Lathrop State Park, home to expansive campgrounds, nearly all of which were empty. Cactus and scrub brush surrounded the peaceful Lake Merriam, where we stopped for a picnic lunch. Deer prints were abundant in the sand surrounding the lake, and spectacular rock formations carved by wind and age circled the water. It was views like this that helped me understand why David liked the place so much. A lone bird swam by slowly, its long-necked silhouette the only break in the long, placid surface of the lake.

I wanted to hike. My legs were itchy for some real exercise after all of our driving, and perhaps motivated by thoughts of David climbing here. Again, I suggested heading to Little Bear. But Mom wasn't up for more than walking, so we wandered around the park for the rest of the afternoon like the lost people we were.

On our last day, we faced the inevitable. We had been behaving like mere tourists, enjoying the scenery, driving many miles around the goal point. It was now or never. But we took it slowly, starting out at the Alamosa Wildlife Sanctuary, from which we had a great, and distant, view of the expansive Sangre de Christos. It gave us a slow approach, a warm up. I edged us closer. We passed the Great Sand Dunes National Park, where people ski on sand as if on snow.

Mom directed and I drove. She remembered the way, and her uneasy look made me assume she was reflecting on her trip from a year before. Having treated our excursion up to this point as though it were a vacation may have been an attempt to ensure this visit was distinctly different than her last.

I turned off the main paved road onto a dirt one so skinny it barely fit our vehicle. It ran through another wide-open expanse of cracked dry earth, sprinkled with a few low bushes and copious quantities of rocks. The mountain range felt like it was coming closer more than that we were approaching it. Dark splotches came into focus revealing themselves as evergreens covering the lower two-thirds of the range, and the peaks loomed above, barren and sharp. I steered the car slowly, almost fearfully, navigating straight toward Blanca Peak, the first David had ascended that day. The road was terrifically bumpy; more than unpaved, it was full of enormous rocks, and we were jostled uncomfortably. I followed the line of a sole barbed-wire fence. Finally, the road became impenetrably rough, and I was afraid I would pop a tire, stranding us out there where I wasn't sure there was cell service. The weather was pristine, so I pulled over and we walked.

This was the course David had traveled on his bright orange mountain bike early in the morning, from a spot where his RV had been parked overnight. I imagined him pedaling along this steep, craggy road, fit for a four-wheel-drive vehicle more rugged than ours with the light of dawn softly illuminating him. I remembered how he clutched those straight handlebars with the tops of his knuckles, and even his thumbs, up. I wondered where he had ditched the bike that day, behind a boulder or something. It seemed hard—in its shock of orange paint—to have been well-camouflaged in this landscape of earth tones.

Mom and I stumbled over the rocks that were now regularly the size of basketballs and bigger as we ascended. We got winded and took breaks, sitting down on tree stumps. At seventy-two, she was fit from yoga classes, but there was a limit to how far we could go. I ached to go higher but knew I wouldn't reach anything lofty, even on my own. When I looked down, it seemed like we'd come a long way, but when I looked up, the peak might as well have been a hundred miles away. I wasn't sure I'd ever felt so puny as I did against the backdrop of that mountain range, in awe of its enormity.

We stopped to take a breath in a clearing on the side of the road, surrounded by aspen trees turning majestically golden in the autumn air. Their heart-shaped leaves cascaded down when the wind blew and freed them from their limbs, and I couldn't help but appreciate that we were being showered in symbols of love. It seemed a good spot to take it all in, meditate, reflect, whatever it was that we intended, if we had intentions; it was serenely quiet and pretty. We had seen no one, so we had as much privacy as we wanted. I sat on a fallen tree and attentively listened to the sound of nothing.

My mother reached into her bag and brought out a cylindrical metal tin, one of the many containers we had purchased at Target in Houston. The sight of it made me cry instantly, as I had no idea she had brought ashes with her on the trip. We had planned little and discussed even less. But now I realized that she might have imagined this moment for some time. I stood next to her, astonished, as she turned toward the bright sky and seemingly spontaneously began to recite "The Road Not Taken" by Robert Frost:

Two roads diverged in a yellow wood,
And sorry I could not travel both
And be one traveler, long I stood
And looked down one as far as I could
To where it bent in the undergrowth;

Then took the other, as just as fair,
And having perhaps the better claim,
Because it was grassy and wanted wear;
Though as for that the passing there
Had worn them really about the same,

And both that morning equally lay
In leaves no step had trodden black.

Oh, I kept the first for another day!
Yet knowing how way leads on to way,
I doubted if I should ever come back.

I shall be telling this with a sigh
Somewhere ages and ages hence:
Two roads diverged in a yellow wood, and I—
I took the one less traveled by,
And that has made all the difference.

Without pause, as if rehearsed, as soon as she spoke her last line, my mother opened the can and released a handful of David's ashes. They were swiftly taken by the wind, drawn upward into a soft swirl, and blown away.

Closer?

How do you rank closeness, if closeness can even be defined? When I considered the quality of David's and my closeness, or ranked our closeness, it only made my insides ache. Even after everything I read, wrote, studied, discussed, and explored, I sometimes felt unentitled to my pain, and spent a lot of time and energy wishing David and I had been a lot closer than we ever were. That we had talked more, seen each other more, done more together, learned more about each other in general. It filled me with regret and longing.

If David and I weren't as close as I wanted us to be, part of what made me extra sad was that I believed each year, we were getting there, slowly but surely. When he died, I hadn't seen him in a while because I hadn't visited Houston since the previous year for Gran's funeral. But during that trip, I had stayed with him at his house, in his guestroom. He and I lingered late over a bottle of wine one night discussing the fact that neither of us wanted to have kids.

"You were my baby," he said. "I don't need any others."

"I was that much trouble, huh?" I grinned.

"Nah, you were good. You were fun."

"I bet I was a pain in the ass."

"Let's just say, I'm all set now." David smiled and hugged me.

Albeit briefly, we lived together again for the first time since we were kids, and we were close.

I like to think that, had he lived, I would have been visiting him more, writing more, calling more, in touch more. But knowing that I couldn't have predicted his death and probably would have assumed, like everyone assumes, that we would have more time, maybe I wouldn't have made more of an effort, maybe I would have taken it all for granted.

I am confident we really did love each other right from the beginning, my beginning, the day I was born. Love counts, right?

And isn't there some intrinsic closeness simply from spilling out of the same womb? Sharing the same mother must count for something. Shared beginnings are unique only to us. Where we came from, our basic origins, on a genetic level as well as a familial one, matter a lot.

I feel great pride owning the same genes he had. When my mother first asked if I wanted any of David's things after he died, I remember saying, "I don't need anything," because at that moment I felt sure we were connected. Even now, I look in the mirror, and though my eyes are a bit greener than his were, the same dense, unruly eyebrows frame them. Our straight, dark brown hair was thick on both of us, and not always easily tamed. Our dimples matched. We really looked like siblings. Especially compared to Tommy, whose own friends didn't buy that we were brother and sister when he showed up with me at a club one time—me: petite, brunette, and olive skinned, next to him: tall, dirty-blonde, blue-eyed, pink-cheeked. They teased us mercilessly, convinced I was his date, which made us both nauseated.

There's something about recognizing another person's voice, too, a sound you know from your earliest memories. David's voice continues to console me when I can summon it, as if replaying a recording in my head. I often fear I'll forget the quality of it, how his tone was smooth and warm. He spoke slowly, as if there was never any hurry. After he died, I called his home phone number just to hear the message, over and over: "Hey, this is Dave... I'm not around, but you might reach me on my cell at 713-587-3511." The way the number rhymed when he said "five eight seven, thirty-five eleven" gave his delivery an especially nice rhythm.

I'll never forget the night nearly a year after he died, in the middle of a work event, when I felt the urgent need to hear the recording, how I went outside to my car for privacy to connect to that touchstone, how I dialed his number again, looking for my quick fix, and how devastated I was to hear that, at last, the service had been disconnected. It took years for me to erase his number from my contacts.

David's visits to my dreams are rare now, and in them he never speaks, but he grins reassuringly at me—sometimes from the far end of a long table. I think this is to demonstrate to me he is okay. I want to tell him I am *not* okay, but I can't reach him—he's too far away, and I don't get the chance before the scene is over. When I wake, I ache for more of his open face, so I squeeze my eyes shut, trying to wind back the dream and play it again to imprint it, but it's so short.

I have gone looking for David in the woods, on top of mountains, canoeing on ponds, in books about cycling and magazines about endurance. I have ached to get closer to him during conversations with his teammates, relatives, colleagues, and friends. I have searched for him by traveling to new places, by working out, pushing myself, taking long walks, going to grad school, taking risks, loving my friends, writing my heart out, going to bereavement groups. I've tried to look at the world considering his perspective, to imagine his lens.

On many occasions, I've actively wondered, in order to try to guide myself, "What would Dave Boyd do?"

Insatiable

I never had a major interest or flair for research, if you could call it that. But after David died, I was ravenous to understand his world and needed—as much as any sustenance—to dig as far as possible in an attempt to uncover the truth about who he was, what he loved, and why. Why not before? I guess I assumed he would always be there to tell me the stories about taking off in the dark in a swamp in a canoe, to be the expert on things like how to read maps and compasses in the middle of a desert, how to sneak in a nap during an adventure race so that you had enough energy but didn't fall behind, and whether one really needed a snakebite kit when roaming through Tasmania. You know, the important stuff.

But in retrospect, I think I couldn't reconcile how vitally important his outdoor adventures were to him and the risks they forced him to take. Getting to know him this way felt critical—if not to make peace with it exactly, then to have greater perspective. Before the accident, I thought of David's pursuits as especially intriguing hobbies, but not holding the weight of a second career. When I was honest with myself, I admit I didn't understand why any of it was worth dying for.

So, I subscribed to *Outside* magazine, which I still read faithfully cover-to-cover each month, as if it's my bible. I've learned about BASE jumping, surfing the biggest waves at Mavericks in California, the youngest female freestyle snowboarder, Nordic skiing in the Alps (plus the way those skiers carry airbags in their gear to save them in case of an avalanche), what it takes to complete the Iron Man World Championships, how difficult a 5.15 climbing route is, the behavior of grizzly bears just below the tree line, where to plan an adventure vacation in Thailand, the best towns in which to live for outdoor activities. I studied how athletes fuel before races and how they pack for major expeditions, what it's like to swim with sharks, kiteboarding basics, the waterfalls in Mexico, and even how to sneak in exercise while sitting at your desk at work.

I regularly review the equipment section near the back to guess which new gadgetry and gear would most excite him: wind and water-proof shells made of high-endurance fabrics; thermal cameras; backpacks sewn together from recycled materials; shoes that can go from mountain to rickshaw to airport to coffee shop to trail run? *What would I buy him for Christmas this year? If he were here. And why didn't I read this magazine before?* If I had, I might have known what to get him for his birthday each year. He was always so hard to shop for.

I've bought so many books about exploits in foreign locales that Amazon and Goodreads continually make suggestions to me in their "you might like" sections for more and different stories of this ilk. I studied Amundson at the South Pole, Krakauer on Everest, Shackleton in Antarctica, Herzog on Annapurna. I consumed books about mountain biking through Ireland, skydiving in the desert, free climbing rock walls, long distance swimming, traveling with sled dogs, walking all of South America, kayaking the rivers of North America, living in ice caves. Collections of essays by Mark Jenkins traveling to places around the globe. Titles like

The Last of His Kind and *Deep Survival*. Women, men, teams, individuals, couples, families. Lots of things David did and plenty he didn't. Anything I thought he'd find intriguing. You name it. I wanted it. I needed it.

I don't actually do any of these things. As Peyton can attest, I was once so exhausted and unhappy on one of our first one-hour hikes that I sat down in the middle of the path and started to cry. I'm better now, but still no real athlete. It doesn't mean I don't appreciate a stunning view or understand the sense of reward from a major accomplishment. But fundamentally, because I don't relate to David in this way, I always found it both interesting and profoundly alien. I suppose that part of me thinks if I fully comprehend what is so compelling about being far away from home, seeing new, interesting landscapes, pushing oneself so hard—pushing oneself to the brink—I will know why it was worth it for him to leave us.

I described myself to someone as "an armchair adventurer" because of this peculiar hobby—or obsession. It makes it easier to explain to others when they see a book about the top female mountaineers in my bag at work.

I used to adore fiction; I ate it up like tasty treats, buried myself in the unreality, savored the escape it provided. Can't stand it now. It all feels so—well, fictional. Made up, unbelievable. So even if the stories aren't about people in the wilderness, my reading choices are now nearly all nonfiction.

Mom, who loves to research and buy books, finally caved and started buying adventure books for me because I wasn't reading any of the fiction she sent. I know she cringed. She acted as though somehow the danger would seep into me, that the thrill-seeking would be contagious, and I would do something insane, like suddenly decide, in my forties, with no background or experience, to go climb K2 alone. Or maybe she just didn't like my obsession. It could also be that she'll never understand my insatiable need to know my brother this way.

For a while, she only bought me books written by and about women and adventure. She gave me *Wild* by Cheryl Strayed before everyone was talking about it; a book by a female author who researched waves—everything from the best surfers to the scientists that study oceanography; and one by Tori Murden McClure, who created her own custom rowboat to cross the Atlantic alone. I loved them.

So, now I know a lot about cols, south-facing vs. north-facing routes, fixed lines, rip cords, crampons, ice axes, saddle bags, crevasses, blood doping, time trials, water purification, shooting Class 5 rapids, fire jumping, even how sea sponges can be used for menstruation. Where has it gotten me?

It got me to this line by Robert McFarlane in *Mountains of the Mind*: "If anyone asks why we mountaineers do it, we do it for the perspicuity." After I looked up "perspicuity" in the dictionary, I stood up and yelled, "Thank you!" out loud to no one. It was something that finally made sense. *Perspicuity: Clarity, lucidity, especially in expression; the state or characteristic of being perspicuous.*

David would have appreciated how—once I picked myself up off the bathroom floor and loosely reassembled the broken pieces of myself that day—the day Mom called and told me that he was dead—my only natural instinct was to grab my dogs and Peyton and immediately hike the closest mountain.

Back to School

After I graduated from Hampshire College when I was twenty-two, David would nudge me to go to grad school off and on. "You know it gets harder and harder to study the longer you're out of practice."

I had no intention of ever getting a master's degree. After having been in school non-stop since I was four years old, I needed a break and assumed I would never want to go back. I was busy playing in a band, writing bad poetry and only slightly better songs, and falling for Peyton. I wasn't at all career-focused and made my rent working alternately at a diner, a post office, and a ceramics studio.

After tendonitis in my wrist from repetitively painting dinnerware forced me to stop playing guitar and working for a while, I found a job at a skin care company as assistant to the creative director, and that was the beginning of my work in marketing and communications, which I still do to make a living. I'm appreciative I found something that still involves putting words together every day, but it's far from the imaginative writing I did as an undergraduate, and, at some point I realized that looking for that kind of satisfaction at my day job wasn't going to cut it.

I joined a couple of local writing groups, but they never quite clicked. I attended workshops here and there and tried to keep writing poems on my own, but the writing only happened in fits and starts. I never found the momentum or support I needed to keep it up. Still, when the thought crossed my mind about going to graduate school for writing, I pushed it aside. I not only figured that ship had sailed long ago, back when a mentor from UMass said he'd happily recommend me for the Iowa Writers Workshop (then and now considered the pinnacle of graduate writing programs), I also asked myself, "What would that possibly do for my career? And how would I ever manage it working full-time?"

When, as a teenager, I told my parents I wanted to write poetry, their one concern was how I would ever make a living. I'd proven now that I could at least support myself, plus I had a musician husband without a "normal" job (i.e. secure), and figured there wasn't room in one relationship for two artists. The practical side of me, worried about health insurance, had nearly killed the truly creative one.

Then David fell off a mountain and died.

It took a few years, but in 2013, I learned about an all-online, non-residential MFA program in creative nonfiction that was starting nearby. I wanted to tell David's story, and I wanted to tell mine—about being his baby sister, about loving him as much as any human on the planet, about our unique relationship, about my heartache and confusion after he was gone, about the real pain of losing a sibling—and I wanted to do it well, in writing. The bereavement-writing group had proven that telling these stories wasn't just therapeutic processing or selfish navelgazing, but that writing and sharing them might be helpful to someone else.

"I heard about this creative writing program," I announced to Peyton one morning over coffee. "I'm seriously thinking of applying."

"I know," he said. "Do you realize you've told me about it ten times already?"

"I have?"

"Yes!" He laughed. "It sounds very cool. Baby, just do it."

My writing sample in my application included twenty pages about my brother's death. I was pleasantly surprised to be quickly accepted into the program. I was even more surprised that workshopping essays about him provoked a reaction beyond sympathy; unlike the former cathartic writing I had done, my classmates' responses made me feel like my words were resonating in a bigger way, that they might have purpose beyond me, and that maybe I really could tell this story. Having begun graduate work thinking that no one else could possibly care about my little life or my losses, my confidence grew along with my skills to do the writing. When a literary journal published an excerpt from my thesis, I felt I might have finally shifted from someone with a story to tell to a storyteller.

I graduated in May of 2016 from Bay Path University, a local women's college with a fledgling MFA program—six classmates and I, who referred to ourselves as guinea pigs, made up their first graduating class. Several chapters of this book were underway, my head was busting with information, and I had a new network of the best writing friends and mentors anyone could ever want. It was indeed hard, as David projected, especially juggling being a full-time student and working full-time simultaneously, plus having been out of school for nineteen years when I started. I'll be paying down the student loans for years. But I did it, and I loved it, and it was entirely worth it whether it ever makes me any money.

Somewhere, I hope, David is proud of me. I'm finding my own perspicuity.

A Place to Sit and Remember

Memorial Park in Houston was originally a training site for World War I soldiers, called Camp Logan. In 1924, after the war, the area was purchased by the philanthropically inclined Hogg family, who then sold it to the city at cost with the specific intention that the land would be turned into a park "in memory of the boys."

Staunch conservationists have protected the grounds from development over the years and ensured that this green space is preserved—no easy feat in an ever-expanding metropolis that thrives on construction and adores concrete. Situated centrally in this fourth largest city in the country, the park boasts a vital natural refuge.

Memorial Park is one of the biggest city parks in America, laying claim to more than 1,500 acres. An arboretum and nature center, which I loved visiting on school field trips as a child, are located on its western edge. Buffalo Bayou, Houston's "river" (really, a man-made concrete trough to ferry rainwater) borders the park on its south side. Freeways frame the other edges. Thirty miles of hiking trails, an acclaimed golf course, picnic areas, playgrounds, sports fields, a swimming pool, running courses, and mountain biking trails are situated right in the heart of an otherwise urban landscape.

Stationed at the entrance of this last amenity is David's memorial bench. From there, one can keep an eye on the comings and goings of the bikers, as they unload their gear from the backs of trucks and SUVs in the parking lot, suit up in streamlined performance wear, and jump on their bikes. These men and women enjoy pedaling through the forested area, just as my brother did when he trained there, rolling up and down hilly, if not exactly mountainous, terrain.

My mother and I are not mountain bikers by any stretch of the imagination. I can't remember the last time she even rode a standard bicycle. But we love to walk, so nearly every time I am in town, we make a pilgrimage to the bench and to the mountain biking trails.

Because there is no grave to visit, this bench is important, functioning much the same way. It not only tells the visiting riders about him, but it also gives us a place to pause and remember. It was an idea Mom came up with, and I will always be grateful to her for it.

The bench is unfussy and sturdy just like David was. A simple steel frame supports six wooden slats, three for the seat and three for the back. The metal plate affixed to the top slat reads:

David Brooks Boyd 1961-2008
Mom, Tommy, and Anne
"My goal in life is to fill every minute of my spare time
with as many fun things outdoors as possible..."

This last line, written by David, was discovered on the Colorado fourteeners website after he died. Glenn, the photographer who had accompanied MOAT on their adventure race the same year, had added underneath, "Mission accomplished!," which I still recall when I need a soothing reminder that he died as he lived, filling every minute of his spare time with as many fun things outdoors as possible.

A lumbering oak tree's branches hang over the bench, providing welcome shade to the sitters beneath. During each visit, I am not only consumed by memories of David, but also by a deep affection, comingled with genuine sorrow, for my mom. Despite being unwilling to weigh one person's grief more heavily than another's, I can't help but think she has suffered more than most. I am my most generous and forgiving toward her at these moments. We stay for a few minutes in quiet reflection, and then we enter the trails.

On a few occasions, we have arrived and found others relaxing on the bench. Irrationally, we are put out, as if these people have encroached on a private space or that they don't appreciate the significance. We have to remind ourselves that we purchased it for sharing.

"Should we ask if they would mind moving for us?" Mom has asked me. When she does, I envision an awkward conversation during which we make innocent strangers uncomfortable. Instead, we change our routine, starting with a walk and hoping the bench will be vacant upon our return.

We choose one or another color-coded path—yellow, purple, or orange—and meander along, exploring, taking our time. Mom has usually put on a cute pair of hipster sneakers like her navy-blue Pumas, along with jeans and a t-shirt. She looks significantly younger than her years and is pretty fit. Her stamina generally matches mine.

In places, the terrain is smooth, hard-packed dirt. In others, where the trails ascend, there are often jutting rocks and steep pitches carved out of the earth, leaving rough embankments where tree roots hang shaggily like badly cut hair. Fallen acorns mingle with sweet gum balls on the ground. Pine and hickory trees draped with vines cluster closely with bushes, forming verdant, tunnel-like passageways.

Occasionally, a biker shouts to alert us of his encroachment. We press to the side of the trail quickly to allow him or her to whizz by and wheel around a curve. It's hard not to envision David at these times, but that's part of why we are here. We know we are a minor annoyance to the bikers, who surely wish we would mosey along other trails not dedicated to them. If we could explain, we would.

There is a spot where one can peer over the bayou, its brown water either rushing or trickling depending on recent rainfall. On the other side is a lavish home replete with an enormous span of green lawn. The first time we saw the menagerie there, we thought our eyes were betraying us, but a donkey, goat, horse, and sheep really do live there, lolling about freely in the sunshine of their palatial habitat, one more element of this park that helps us pretend we aren't surrounded by the city's skyscrapers. I wonder whether David ever took a break here. I know he would have enjoyed the unexpected surprise of farm animals in the city.

Wildlife in the park is evident more by remnants we discover than their living presence. One time, we came across several bones and pieces of the armored shell of an armadillo. Another time, we nearly stepped on a whole skull from an unknown animal with a long snout, fangs, and a tuft of light-colored fur still attached. This specimen was still fragrant in its last throes of decomposition. A possum? Raccoon? We wonder. How long had it been dead? David would surely have had an opinion based on his medical background.

Mom and I recognize certain plants and trees and puzzle over others. "Is that a yaupon with those red berries?" she more or less asks herself. "Ah, ligustrum," she says, pointing to a shiny leafed bush. "I wonder if those would work in the backyard." She is a big leaf collector and usually heads home with a fistful of different shapes. Now I am reminded of David's biology classes while he was an undergrad at the University of Texas. He filled pages of notebooks with drawings of stems and leaves and used to walk me around our backyard making identifications and carefully pronouncing the Latin names of plants, making even weeds seem exceptional. If there had been any money in botany, he might have ended up in that scientific profession.

Dead trees are abundant in the park since the severe drought in 2011. Gloomy brown figures stand like scarecrows along the edges of the jogging trail. Their trunks pile up like corpses in the picnic areas, next to outdoor grills. Places where the canopy was once so dense the sky was all but hidden from view look like a giant punched a hole in the roof.

David didn't ever see this. For him, the park is still as forested as ever. For us, the devastation reminds us of everything we've lost.

We circle back to the parking lot, knowing we will return again next year, and the next, and the next. I hope the bench is durable enough to last forty-seven years, as David did. I will be an old woman then, older than Mom is now, coming to rest at this spot to remember a fascinating man I had the honor of knowing, of loving. I'll feel like his baby sister again for a few minutes.

As I sit, I'll watch the young people come to the trails and check out the incredible new gear they will surely have then. I'll recall how David taught me about cyclocross racing and time trials, the way he outfitted his team with the most current, highest performing equipment. I'll watch as this new generation mounts their bikes and adventures off into the woods, wishing he could be there with me.

Words with Tommy

One Sunday evening, I tucked myself into bed earlier than usual with the intention of getting a long night's rest before the busy workweek ahead. Per my usual routine, in my self-mothering way, I told myself not to open any social media apps. I would just catch up with my Words with Friends games and then go straight to sleep.

Once under the covers, I tapped the big golden "W" icon on my iPhone and opened the first of two games I almost always have going with Tommy. He plays under the name "Fastloaner," an identity borne from his business persona. It's a moniker he uses for his email address as well and probably any number of other things I don't know about—one that reminds me of how he's been a slick businessman all his life, starting out by earning salesman-of-the-month awards as a teenager selling subscriptions to the *Houston Chronicle* over the phone.

Once, over dinner at Mom's, Tommy regaled the family with a story about how he had camped out at a car dealership all day long, wheeling and dealing to ensure that Alison got the best possible deal, better than the best deal any Joe Schmo could ever expect, a deal so great no normal customer would ever be able to get it. His blue eyes lit up while he spoke, as he recalled how much he pushed, how the salesperson pulled, what a game it all was, how he won, and he won big.

It sounded about as fun to me as swallowing nails, but he loved every minute of it. For Tommy, negotiation and strategizing come so naturally, they're like breathing, and success is like the adrenaline-fueled breath a runner experiences crossing the finish line ahead of the rest of the pack.

When we discovered that we both loved Words with Friends one Christmas five years ago, I was very surprised. "*You* play Words with Friends?" I remember asking in my condescending little sister voice.

This was not my academically achieving brother, David. This is the one who got all Cs in school (when he was lucky). I never think of him as an intellectual, never mind a "word person."

I, on the other hand, was the artist in the family, studying creative writing since fourteen, penning long, descriptive poems that I shared with my best friend in the high school hallways, poring over our lines scrawled on college-rule pages torn out of notebooks and folded in our pockets like secret treasures. I was madly in love with the dictionary and read books like they were nourishment. I had gone to a college based almost exclusively on the fact that I could major in creative writing there. *I* was the word person. I *am* the word person. Surely Tommy, of all people, was a joke at this game. I would whip his butt, and it would be so satisfying.

"Bring it on," I said at his invitation to play.

It turns out that strategy is as much a factor in winning Words with Friends as a knowledge of actual words, perhaps more. For months, I would seethe when Tommy played words that I knew he couldn't possibly define. In Scrabble, our analog childhood version of the game, he would never have pulled it off.

He'd end up showing me his hand with all the toying around he did before committing to a play. And if he tried to play an unknown word, I would have challenged him to define it and he would have balked. But in Words with Friends, given the time, he could move letters around as much as he liked without my seeing them to find out whether the computer brain would allow his play. He could also spend time figuring out how to land on double and triple letter spaces rather than focusing on creating interesting words, emphasizing *where* he played, not what he played. He usually tried to maximize what's there by positioning the word so that it actually created not one, but two—or even three—words with just one turn, therefore racking up tons of points on dumb little two- and three-letter terms purely because of placement.

This was very disappointing to me. Having my brother beat me swiftly at a game I felt destined to win was embarrassing. It brought out the worst in me.

I would push the small screen on my phone into Peyton's face and say, "Look at that! I am *positive* Tommy doesn't know what GLAIR means. *I* don't even know!" He would sigh deeply, rolling his eyes, as I looked up the word on my Merriam-Webster app, it having replaced my heavy paper dictionary long ago, and would pronounce the word to mean "a sizing liquid made from egg white."

"Ugh, he's an idiot."

"It's a *game*," Peyton would remind me.

I would message Tommy through the little chat function in the game over and over when I found his choices of plays ridiculous: *Do you even know what ADZ means??* or *OKAPI?? That's an S.A.T. word for sure, smarty!* Or *ZA? That's not a word! That's a ridiculous abbreviation for pizza!*

My snottiness had no effect on him whatsoever. *Well, it played!* He'd write back. *Big bro having fun!!!* It was maddening.

For months, in an act of sheer superiority, I decided to teach him when he played words I knew he didn't know, messaging the definitions to him as if I would somehow be expanding his vocabulary, at least. He didn't care. He wasn't interested.

That Sunday night, cozy in bed, I opened the first game and scanned the grid. It was a newer set-up with just a few words played so far—benign, simple ones like GLOB, MUG and YE. In the bright yellow digital tile letters, Tommy had set up one of his usual moves, capitalizing on creating three words at once: MET and YA along with the overarching play, MOAT.

My breath caught.

That short little word was one that I had been able to play many times over the many years and countless games, but deliberately chose not to. For most people, it is a word with no hidden meaning, just a term out of a fairy tale—describing a protective trench of water surrounding a castle, maybe filled with alligators, maybe with a dragon behind a drawbridge—but it obviously means something else to Tommy and me, and he had never played it before.

I was glad I was by myself in bed. Socially, triggers were so inconvenient—those strange, uncomfortable secrets gave me odd bursts of interior pain that usually had to be stifled for the comfort of others. I had been known to duck into bathroom stalls at work, close doors at home, and pop inside the protective bubble of my car to experience moments too private and hard to explain or experience in front of coworkers, friends, even Peyton.

One tiny four-letter word shouldn't set me off so much after six years, should it? Was it reasonable for this to be a trigger at this late date? What is reasonable anyway?

Seeing the word sent me immediately back to all of David's races in a swirl of places: Utah, Montana, Louisiana, Florida, South Dakota, Costa Rica, Colorado, Tasmania, Texas, Greenland. I thought about all the times Mom and I had followed the team's courses online—as they stopped at checkpoints, we delighted in pictures, triumphed with them when they pulled ahead, struggled with them when they fell behind. We tracked them during races as they crossed mountains, kayaked rivers, swam across ponds, ran through deserts, biked across plains, rode horses across meadows. I sensed she was always a little white knuckled when we checked in with each other over his seven- or ten- or fourteen-days trips. Though she didn't tell me as much, I had the feeling she didn't sleep well during those expeditions because I know she checked the website almost constantly. Her nerves showed when she emailed me at work all day, every day while he was on a course.

Occasionally we watched the little dot, marking their spot on a map, move in the wrong direction, which panicked us, but they ultimately corrected their errors and crossed the finish line. They never didn't finish, like so many other teams, who dropped out because of injury or fatigue or the ensuing delirium, or poor judgment, or a combination of all of these. We rooted for them, shared our excitement as they moved up leaderboards, and sighed deep, deep breaths of relief when MOAT finished.

I still believe David was never afraid. Maybe that isn't true—just my larger-than-life version of him—but I never witnessed an inkling of fear. The only thing close was a confession he made to Mom about one time he was genuinely worried about his team, but that was him thinking about other people, not himself, as usual.

The word, his team's name, also made me think again about his teammates, the second family he had, the one he loved as much as us, maybe more. The ones he not only competed with, but traveled with, ate meals with, slept with, made life and death decisions with. There is a great photo of all the various members of MOAT who competed, arms around each other, all wearing sporty tops emblazoned with the name of their team in chunky dramatic font-face as if MOAT were a band. As if they were wearing concert tees. I remembered how after David's death they decided to change the name temporarily to iMOAT, to stand for the words, "In Memory of a Teammate." What a tribute. iMOAT stickers were made up and passed around at his memorial service along with the orange wristbands. It's been years since mine peeled off the back of my car.

Tommy invited me to play my first Words with Friends game with him that Christmas day five years ago and we never stopped. In fact, we barely pause. Peyton thought it might be a cute phase, but it has become an integral part of my every day. I genuinely can't imagine life without it.

Now I am just grateful we have this mechanism in place that keeps us together. We don't often talk on the phone or even email; this is it for regular communication. At least I know he's there on the other end somewhere every day. Occasionally, Mom will tell me that she hasn't heard from him in a month, and I'll say, "He's alright. He played me in Words with Friends today." Checking in with him in this way assures me that we are connected, even though we may not be very close in any other way.

Occasionally, he sends me a message like *Ouch!* if I play a really good one, and I momentarily allow myself to feel like a rock star, but he is more likely to speak up with something chest-puffingly confident like, *Keep 'em coming! I'm having a GREAT time!* if my playing is sucking particularly badly. The competitive spirit is alive and well with him. Sometimes, I actually tell myself that I am letting him win because it matters so much more to him. He is, after all, the only truly competitive one left now.

I didn't message Tommy about his use of the word MOAT in his play in Words with Friends that night. I knew he thought about that combination of letters as he moved the electronic pieces into place; there was no way he hadn't. I left it unspoken and went ahead and placed my tiles, creating the word HUH in response. It spoke plenty between us.

Higher, Farther, Faster

"Why would someone want to do that?" my mother asked. She was sitting at my dining room table and had opened my new issue of *Outside* magazine to a full-page glossy picture of a guy in a kayak hurtling at the speed of God-knows-what down a gushing waterfall. He seemed to be hovering just above the spray, paddle suspended, as he careened nose-first over the white crashing waves.

It's the kind of question my mother asks about a lot of things. It would have annoyed me even if it were being posed in terms of why someone would want to be a politician or listen to heavy metal or wear the color yellow. *Why does anyone want to do anything, Mom?* I wanted to say, using my most teenaged voice. I never quite know if she is being rhetorical or whether she really expects an answer. But it was extra vexing in this case. Asking that question about an adventurous athlete encapsulated so much that she had avoided and I had stared at, as if unable to look away, for years.

"Didn't you know your son at all?" I asked, bristling. I didn't consider how vicious it might sound until it was said. Once the words spilled out of my mouth, I wished I could take them back. It was, in fact, precisely the question I had been trying to answer ever since David's accident.

To my mother, this was an illustration of illogical risk-taking. It didn't make sense to her why anyone would do something that so clearly taunted death. We both knew from experience that the expensive helmet he was wearing wouldn't save him if he were pinned under the water or got knocked out by a rock or the current became too swift and he lost control. She saw this two-dimensional stranger, and I imagined she imbued him with selfishness, lack of awareness or consideration of others, perhaps a mental instability. I pictured her mind catapulting straight to thoughts of his parents, his wife, his children, his teammates, his siblings?—and even the photographer taking this picture—who would be forever traumatized should he end up injured, paralyzed, or dead.

Despite my guessing at her thoughts, she gave little away. I watched her face: skin softened a little with age, pink lips pursed. Her gaze was steady on the page, as if she was reading, though there wasn't more than a short caption. Her stoicism never ceases to amaze me.

To David, this would have been a perfect visual definition of the word "thrill." It's the kind of image that I think captured his imagination for most of his life and part of what propelled him into the world of athletic competition and outdoor adventure.

Despite the question, my mother doesn't really delve into that psychology, doesn't study it like I do, like it's my job.

Fundamentally, David was terribly curious. He always wanted to see something different, experience the unknown, try another discipline, challenge himself in a new way. Uncharted territory seemed to be the quest. Like all extreme athletes, he also wanted to push himself to achieve more and always to do it better and faster.

We were a pretty active family—riding bikes, playing tennis, shooting hoops, and skiing. My brothers both played soccer at the YMCA. But David took athleticism so much farther than anyone else. When he attended medical school in Galveston, he got his first taste of multi-disciplinary racing and training by doing a bunch of triathlons: he was running, cycling, and swimming alongside and right in the waters of the Gulf of Mexico.

The next thing we knew, all of his free time was spent traveling and taking on new physical challenges: scuba diving in Mexico, bone fishing in the Christmas Islands, trekking in Iceland. He was so accomplished that he was once featured on the cover of *Runner Triathlete News*. In the photo, he's making a hilariously avid face as though he's yelling, "Yeah!" at the top of his lungs while gripping the handlebars of his mountain bike tightly and barreling down a slope as fast as he can.

When David found adventure racing, it must have been like falling in love. Such a variety of disciplines to master plus managing gear, planning travel, organizing a support team, learning new landscapes, watching the weather, and ultimately racing while orienteering through rugged, potentially hazardous, places; tending to injuries, strategizing sleep, handling food intake, and leading a group of equally avid teammates. It sounds like a torture test to most of us, but I knew he lived for it. I supposed his excellent run of contests culminated rather nicely at Primal Quest in Montana, where MOAT did so well, where Glenn finally captured them on film.

I don't know for sure, but after all my reading, I imagined that the fact that death is just around the corner could actually be a motivator in these settings, whether consciously or not. Cheating it is its own thrill. Titles like *Addicted to Danger* have taught me a lot. There was clearly something addictive about the rush David experienced competing athletically, and especially when he was attempting to conquer The Great Outdoors at the same time. Adding white water, jagged rocks, and high altitude to the equation usually provided a background at once dangerously beautiful and exciting.

Maybe I should have been concerned, but this was my big brother; I assumed he was invincible. And there was never any question of trying to stop him from doing it—he had always been on his own journey and his fervor seemed to grow each time he stumbled on a new sport or location to explore. We lost track of his trips and races, there were so many. He was always training for something. It became the norm for him to arrive at 8:30 a.m. for Christmas breakfast at Mom's house and tell us he had done a ten-mile run before he arrived.

The next morning, Mom came into my room just as I was waking up and plopped down on my bed as if this was some regular, cozy routine, though she was visiting for the first time in over a year. Noticing the stacks of books surrounding me, she reached out to one on top of my nightstand.

"They wrote a whole book about this?" she asked. I looked up and realized she was holding a mid-sized paperback called *Colorado 14er Disasters*.

"David's in there, you know," I said as if it was an answer. Her nosing around always irked me, but this discovery felt especially invasive. I wondered why I kept it out in plain sight, though it wasn't a secret.

"He is?" She sounded stunned. Her eyes were initially wide and then her brows furrowed as she opened the cover.

"Yeah. Shaun told me about it. I think Patti told him."

I tensed up, feeling her distrust emanate through the room. Should I have told her? It hadn't even occurred to me.

"Well, I find it interesting no one told *me*," she said with a tone I recognized from the many times she had acted slighted, betrayed, or left out, especially when it came to me and my siblings. I was forty-two years old but felt like a little kid in trouble. "Where did they get their information?"

"I don't know," I answered quickly, which was true. Then, I actually wondered: *Who is this Mark Scott-Nash, the author? Did he talk to our brother Tommy? Were the details reported to him by search and rescue? Why had I had simply accepted the information without question?* "Do you want me to show you the passage where he appears?"

"I don't know," she said back to me and started thumbing through the pages anyway.

I continued to sit in bed next to her as she went silent, flipping through black and white photos of mountain passes, stopping at chapter headings. I felt pinned in and not quite awake enough to know what to do. It was like she had stumbled on some secret, though I'd been completely up-front with her about my interest in digging into David's death.

"Well, there's an error right there!" she announced triumphantly, pointing to a page.

"Really? What is it?"

"They got the date wrong. It says he was found on September fourth, and it was the fifth." She was right.

The book had been the only document I had to go on that was specific to David; it was the only record that provided any details about the accident because no one was with him when he fell. And I knew there was initial confusion about his date of death because of when he had fallen versus when he had been discovered. I had used this book as a research tool to help make sense of what happened—or at least understand what *might* have happened.

As I sat there in bed, I remembered when I had ordered the book a few months back. I remembered the anticipation and wondering what it would contain. I remembered bringing it upstairs to this same bed and hungrily opening it, looking for "David Boyd" in the table of contents and then flipping to the back, hoping for an index that wasn't there. It took me some time to locate him on page eighty-seven in the middle of a chapter aptly titled, "Solo," since this was one of the few trips he took alone. I remembered how Peyton had come into my room just as tears started to stream down my cheeks in a way I couldn't control.

"Can I read this to you?" I had asked him. It felt ever-so-slightly safer with him there as a sort of witness. He stood in the doorway with an expression I had seen many times over the years—equal parts helpless and nervous, sad and loving—and not answering, though he was hardly in a position to deny my request. This was perhaps *the* book I'd been looking for as I read those dozens and dozens of other stories.

I launched into it, though from the start, I struggled over each paragraph, choking through the recap of David's journey, sobbing with a force that I hadn't experienced in a long, long time.

"Boyd's ambitious plan was well within his athletic ability," I read. "He was a regular participant in hundred-mile biking and running endurance events. He had climbed forty of the four-teeners already…"

I continued: "Boyd summited Blanca Peak, a relatively straight-forward trail hike, signed the summit register and progressed to Ellingwood Point … then descended back to the basin below the ramparts of Little Bear Peak." It was like watching a movie you've seen before many times and knowing how it ends yet hoping—beyond all reason—that it will be different this time. He won't fall. He won't die.

I have a picture of David and his teammates standing on a massive rock outcropping in Australia where everyone is sitting down safely as David is perched on a small point holding his arms up in a V like he just made a touchdown. He looks as happy as I ever saw him. But I envisioned his peak bagging wouldn't have always ended with one of these postures if he was alone, thus I conjured up the selfie I had seen on his laptop back at Tommy's house when I thought of him reaching the apex of Little Bear.

The author went on to describe the challenging parts of the final climb, which my brother managed apparently without issue, further confounding all of us. Because of where he was found, Scott-Nash wrote, it seemed that "he had negotiated the most notorious pitches of Little Bear only to succumb on the relatively simple lower slopes, apparently trying to descend the west ridge too early, mistaking a steep, cliff-like couloir for the easy exit further down the ridge …"

It was almost too hard to read. But it revealed details I didn't know, and I was still so ravenous for information. "There are at least two explanations for Boyd's apparent lapses in judgment." This phrase alone was gutting. Anyone who ever knew him was

---

aware that David didn't have lapses in judgment. "The first was his physical state ... He had expended an exorbitant amount of energy at altitudes above 13,000 feet ... It is likely Boyd was not at 100 percent decision-making capacity ... The second explanation is that he may have been caught in a storm ..." The latter was the one formal theory that had been bandied around in the immediate aftermath, and it was one that I had clutched because I simply couldn't imagine him, under any circumstances, making such a terrible mistake.

Something about the accident documented in black and white made it real all over again. It was almost like learning about it for the first time. I had bit my lip to try to control my crying and held onto Peyton tightly, as if he was a life raft.

Now I braced for my mother's reaction as she continued to read, maybe hoping for one? But her expression never changed through the entire chapter, and she said nothing else. She simply put the book back on top of the others where it had been and left the room.

Danger and Desire

Casually skimming news on my phone while hanging out on the couch with Peyton after work, I read about Dean Potter, a name I recognized from my adventure reading, and found out he had died over the weekend. Potter was a BASE jumper, of all things, a man who wore a wingsuit and acted like some sort of superhero leaping off cliffs. During one of his many bigger flights, though not a stunt outside his regular purview, he and his partner ended up face down on the rocks in Yosemite National Park. I was anything but shocked. Isn't it only a matter of time for a BASE jumper? I mean, come on. That's just tempting fate. I shook my head as I told Peyton, who only sighed, surely ready for me to move on. Another amazing adventurer gone. Just like David. And another devastated family.

BASE jumping seems sort of ridiculous—my mother would find it insane—and yet, these athletes have a dedication and focus that is hardly found elsewhere. They experience things we never will. It's easy to call them crazy, but that's so dismissive. Is it just because we don't have that drive that we can't relate? Or are our chosen passions just so much safer? I've grown impressed with both the tenacity required and the serious dedication these people have to themselves and their passions.

I also continued to feel furious and profoundly sad. I could assume that's precisely what Potter's friends and family were feeling right then, mixed with their admiration and love. I could practically hear them trying to reassure themselves by saying things like, "Well, he died on his own terms." "At least he was doing what he loved." And "It's the way he would have wanted to go out." They would all be right. And it would still suck.

As much as I adored David for being unapologetically himself to the very end, my body flooded with resentment when I thought about the mess he made. Not only did the loss crush us with grief, dying without a will made for a six-year legal disaster and the ravaging of his substantial estate, it destroyed relationships among family members, and left me and Tommy feeling utterly abandoned. Worst of all, he left us with a fundamentally unsolvable mystery, try as I did to find answers.

The stories I read illustrated the early drive for daredevil stunts. Some of these colorful characters were babies climbing the rails of their cribs. I could imagine Potter doing that. Certainly, my brother was always brave and inquisitive, from his early water-skiing days to high school chemistry experiments gone wrong. I suppose the sense of immortality that most of us feel when young could have hooked into these guys (and girls) in a more permanent way. Maybe it's something innate, like genetics.

David wasn't unscathed by his exploits. In fact, he got hurt a lot, and, in retrospect, seemed to have nine lives, like proverbial cats do. A nasty motorcycling accident early on and falling asleep behind the wheel on the freeway could have killed him either time. On an old postcard sent from Mexico he wrote, "I've been having a great time scuba diving, even though I got bitten by a moray eel my second day here." Mountain biking in the jungles of Costa Rica, dodging low-hanging vines to a soundtrack of the calls of exotic birds while on his mountain bike, he had a dramatic crash. I stared wide-eyed as he described the resulting gash in his arm and a trip to a local hospital, at which he lost his patience waiting for treatment and sewed up his own wound. There were a number of other stiches and broken bones along the way. All in a day's, or a life's, adventure.

Why push the limit? Potter said in an article in *Outside*, "I stay well within my abilities and never go to those places that are too harsh to handle." I bet David felt that way too, even as he took on not one, but fifty-four 14,000-foot peaks when he had never done anything like it. I know these men weren't the same, but the fundamental mentality behind what they loved more than anything was identical.

I later heard a piece on NPR about Potter's accident. The interviewer spoke to a close friend and suggested, as gently as possible, that maybe this wasn't totally surprising? No. Dean's friends were shocked too. Because, like David, he was so fit, so prepared, so experienced. I watched his partner, Graham Hunt, on YouTube recording his thoughts after his mentor died BASE jumping saying, "I have to believe that we don't have to die doing this." Sigh.

Soon after, news suggested that Potter was wearing a GoPro camera on his helmet when he went down. I was amazed and horrified that someone could watch his fatal collision with the ground, especially from his point of view. Part of me is like anyone who can't stop from rubbernecking at a car crash—I almost wished, in the sickest way, that I would be able to see it. Maybe someone would stream it online because we have no boundaries anymore. Then I was glad when I couldn't find it, alongside feeling a little ashamed for looking. But mostly, I felt a certain kind of peace about the fact that this recording might have existed because it could offer an explanation, at least, to his girlfriend, his mom, and his sister. And maybe because I would have an inkling of what my brother experienced.

I don't know why knowing what happened in these awful situations is helpful, but it often is. What we will never know about David's fall continues to haunt. Despite the GPS noting his location, the signed log books, the study of where he was found, there are answers we will never have.

My curiosity persisted. One day at work, I Googled "author Mark Scott-Nash" and was surprised when I easily found him on LinkedIn. I sent him a message through his account (what the hell) and was amazed at his responsiveness. Within a matter of hours, we had scheduled a phone date.

In preparation, I read more about him and learned he is both an accomplished mountaineer and a search and rescue guy. I put together a few interview-ish questions, just in case. When Mark called, I was surprised by how high his voice sounded. After a few introductory niceties, I launched right into the story about my mom picking up his book.

"So where *did* you get your information? Were you on my brother's SAR?" I hoped that using the abbreviation for search and rescue made me sound more knowledgeable than I was.

"No," he answered, and I was relieved. I had considered this possibility before we spoke and thought that might be too intimately close. "And I didn't know your brother. But I knew the guys on his SAR. I talked to them, and I talked to people who were on the mountain that day." Close enough.

He told me that he was inspired to write the book after telling others about accidents in the mountains over beers. They were interesting stories, he said, and because people often make the same mistakes, he hoped lessons might be learned. David's accident just happened to occur while he was in the middle of writing the collection, and that was why his fateful journey was included.

Mark described Little Bear's topography for me since he had climbed it four times himself. The couloir leading to the summit funnels a lot of spontaneous rock fall along with moisture from recent rain, snow, or ground water. Every time he had climbed it, it was wet. He thought David's note in the register at the summit, *Nice & Dry!* might have referred to this section more than the weather in general. He told me about being caught in a hailstorm there, and that conditions are changeable within an hour.

"The best climbers in the world have accidents," he assured me. "I consider myself very, very lucky. I've had many close calls."

This statement provoked my pinnacle question: "So, Mark. Let me ask you, why do you do it?"

"There are a lot of reasons. It's a compelling lifestyle. If you love the outdoors and are strong enough to climb the mountains, it's a personal accomplishment. You also get a lot of reinforcement and admiration. The ego thing—it's there," he admitted. "But it's also the whole experience, the singular focus, the involvement of your entire self. Mountaineering involves all the parts of me, nature and the environment, and being part of it. It's also an intellectual thing—making decisions, in an expedition, all of the things you have to put together. It's a visceral experience in life that you don't get anywhere else."

"But what about the risk?"

"Risk is part of the whole experience," he says. "You're beating it."

Our conversation, so direct and honest and clear on both of our parts, gave me a little peace, a little more understanding, a little extra closeness to my brother, but I wondered how it would make my mother feel.

Part of me wished she would just fall apart already to demonstrate that she was as emotional, as broken, as human as I was. Was it possible that her grief was so immense that removing her finger from the dam could drown her?

Reorientation

Nearly seven years after David's death, I took Trixie for a walk around the block in my neighborhood feeling a lasting gratitude that he had given me his blessing of sorts to have this dog join our family. It was a clear, cool evening, my favorite kind of early summer weather in New England. I looked westward and noticed the North Star even though I wasn't intentionally looking for it.

But wait a minute.

It was the North Star, after all—so, wasn't it supposed to appear in the *north* not the *west*? It occurred to me that I had no idea despite thinking I knew about stars. I've always been an embarrassment at understanding geography and only knew that the direction I faced was west because Peyton had told me when we moved into our house a couple of years prior. Still, this star's location should have been obvious because of the name—this wasn't rocket science. When I got home, I Googled "North Star position." Before I could figure out where this brilliant speck of light was supposed to appear in the sky, I read, "The North Star, also known as Polaris, is located in the constellation of Ursa Minor, the Little Bear."

Ooh. After all this time, I had never made the connection between my personal symbol for David and this name. Little

Bear, where he last wrote his name. Little Bear, where he either became disoriented or got caught in a storm, where he went the wrong way, the only time he ever got lost. Little Bear, a name that should be cute, but never can be.

Once I digested this new information, further online research showed that the North Star should indeed be found in the northern sky. Duh. "At the North Pole, this pinpoint of light is directly above the viewer." The North Star apparently always appears to have spilled out from the cup of the Big Dipper, one of the only formations I have been able to recognize since I was a child lying on that pier over the lake in East Texas. The North Star makes the end point of the handle of the Little Dipper. And it's not the brightest star anyway. It actually ranks forty-eighth in brightness, only a "medium luminosity" in the world of stars. Still, because of its absolute position in the north, it continues to be considered a critical beacon, and being able to find it is a basic survival skill. Something David surely had no problem doing from anywhere on the globe.

What I'd been looking at all this time was most likely not a star at all, but a planet, Mars. Everything I read indicated that it is bright and obvious and to be found glowing in the west. I had to laugh at myself.

The symbols and rituals, the things we think we know, the things we think we see, are intended to help us navigate and reorient us in the world. As it happens, I'm no astronomer, and my spirituality is as muddled as ever. I'm still trying to figure out how to live without David, and what I believe in.

I'm just facing west—from here, it's where my amazing brother was last, physically, in relation to where I am. It's where the sun sets, where we say goodbye to each day. Maybe I should reconsider David as the sun, truly the brightest star.

"David Brooks?"

I was sitting in the radiology department of our local hospital with Peyton, who was there for X-rays of his back. He'd been in ongoing pain for a couple of months, and we weren't sure what discovery might be made, but neither of us believed it was going to be anything good, so we were edgy.

I flipped through the magazines on the side table distractedly. Scanning my phone wasn't any more captivating. Peyton was so uncomfortable just sitting in the waiting room chair. He wasn't even talking, and I couldn't find anything interesting to entertain him with. I wanted to hold hands, but that's my kind of comfort, not his.

Hospitals make me uncomfortable on a good day. Their sticky sweet fragrance of sick comingling with disinfectants always makes me feel unwell. After waiting half an hour, I started griping about how many patients seemed to be ahead of us despite our carefully scheduled and honored appointment.

Eventually, a tech donning classic cornflower blue scrubs emerged from the back, we looked over, and she called out, "Mr. Brooks? Mr. David Brooks?"

It's a name, just a name. Except to us. Jesus, why is the universe alternately kind and horrible?

Ever since David died, seeing anyone, anywhere, wearing scrubs automatically made me wince, and since we were in the radiology department, it made me feel even worse to start with. Now this woman asked for a patient who had his first and middle name. It was a perfect storm. I sucked in a quick breath and held it, trying to stay calm. I looked over at Peyton for reassurance, and he was expressionless, obviously having missed the name.

"David Brooks?" she said again, more loudly, as if to hurt me intentionally.

I exhaled and tried to breathe evenly. Still Peyton didn't notice.

The man in question finally stood. He was tiny and old and wrinkly—not to mention clearly hard of hearing—and looked nothing at all like my brother. But it didn't matter. The damage was done.

I hadn't braced myself for tears that day. I just went to support my husband, who was scared about the throbbing of his back. Instead, I received this emotional fist to the cheek when I never saw the punch being thrown. Now I was the one who needed care.

Gone for seven years, and the sense of loss slapped me afresh. It felt as though I had gotten the call from Mom the day before. "They found his body," only this side of the phrase, "Your brother is dead."

I was so tired of the triggers by that point, the surprise attacks that doomed my composure. How I wished those moments would upset me less, always inconveniently timed. I averted my eyes from the techs tormenting me in their scrubs and practiced slow breathing.

My mind drifted to the famous news commentator, David Brooks, who comes on NPR regularly to give a perspective on current political events from his Republican side of things. Our mother adores him, despite being intensely left leaning. She'll say casually, "I heard David Brooks on the radio today ... he's really so smart," as if the name doesn't mean anything, and I wonder if she somehow doesn't make the connection or refuses to let it touch her. But it's the same name she must have worked over in her mind while she was pregnant with our David Brooks. Why doesn't she flinch?

Now that my brother is gone, it seems wrong that anyone else could bear his name. It's like a ball player's number that should be retired.

There was a floodgate that wanted to be pushed open. Part of me needed to hold it shut, and part of me wished I could let it rush all over me, pulling me under where I could submerge myself in my grief again. But that really wasn't the time or place. Even if Peyton had heard the tech, he wouldn't know I wanted him to put his arm around me. It had been so long, after all. In those situations, I was obliged to console myself.

In the waiting room, I gave way to exactly two tears, carefully wiped away on a sleeve before he noticed. Another tech appeared, eyes scanning the room, and said brightly, "Mr. Peyton Pinkerton?"

Talk About It

Tommy finally confessed to me that he had always kept busy—inordinately busy—with his work, kids, and girlfriend. With golfing, hunting, and traveling, anything in order to keep himself from ruminating, anything to keep him feeling sane. I occasionally received a sweet text message late at night while he was likely drinking and allowing himself to feel his feelings, but usually, he made sure to be as distracted as possible from the reality of losing David.

That admission happened only after he'd found a great new therapist. I was proud of him for doing that, only guessing at the magnitude of what he must have been going through for years. I sensed he was constantly vigilant to push the agony away into a dark corner, pretending not to be able to see it, but feeling its hideous presence whenever he was alone. Bringing it out into the light after so long was necessary in the long term, but it seemed terrible in the short term. I think it took a long time for Tommy to realize that ignoring his grief wouldn't work and was even compounding it over time. Even the kids were going to therapy at last—Christopher and Emily, who had not only had to say goodbye to their Uncle Dave, but also to their parents' marriage that same year, were certainly overdue for some help with processing it all.

Tommy, his girlfriend, Stacy, and I were having dinner at a high-end restaurant in downtown Houston that he had chosen. I was happy to be with them enjoying delicious food and glass after glass of wine, and talking about David in open, honest, loving terms. I told them about my writing and what it had done for me in terms of trying to make sense of our brother's death and the ways it was providing meaningful connections with others, even strangers, by talking about it.

"I want to read your stuff," Stacy said.

"Really?" No one in the family had *ever* asked to read anything by me. Once, Mom had even come right out and said to me, "I'd like to read your writing, but it would make me too sad." I wasn't sure whether Stacy was just being kind.

"Yes!" Stacy said.

"Some of it's dark, you know," I told her. "But you are welcome to check it out."

"I really want to," she confirmed.

While we picked at our meals, I told her and Tommy more: about my MFA program and professors, about the areas of David's life I'd been researching, about the *Colorado 14er Disasters* book. Tommy got up suddenly and left the table. Stacy and I kept talking. When my brother returned a few minutes later, his eyes were red. He was trying so hard not to, but he started crying again, tears plopping on the white tablecloth.

I went around the table and put my arms around him. As he wept, he finally let me sit in his lap, and I held him there, not caring whether we were making a scene. As my tough six-foot-four brother got my shoulder all wet, I didn't cry; I was, in fact, delighted. It was the sweetest moment Tommy and I had ever had, at least since childhood. It was the vulnerable opening with him that I had craved for so long. He was letting me take care of him for a minute, he allowed himself to hurt, and I was grateful.

The waiters kindly gave us a wide berth for a while. Tommy said he thought it would be helpful for the two of us to go to counseling together, and I was sincere when I said I would do it in a heartbeat if I lived in town, and even that we could arrange something for my next visit if he wanted to.

We picked at dessert, drank a final glass of wine, and—after nearly three hours—finally got up to leave. When he hugged me goodbye, Tommy said, "You can put this in your book."

I wrote Stacy that night: *You are a champ to take any part in this family story. Since you were so kind to ask, here's the piece we talked about at dinner.* I attached one of the longer chapters I'd been working on, a fifteen-pager, thinking that would give her a lot to chew on.

By the time I woke up the next morning, she had already responded: *I read it. I need more :)* She continued, *I was so moved, and I need to read it two or three more times to memorize the details. It's so good! There were two or three phrases you used that spoke to me on a very deep level.*

You're kidding, I wrote back. *You're just being nice.*

I couldn't stop reading it once I started, she insisted. *I think I went to sleep around 2 am. But I wanted to see where it was going so, please send more when you are ready to share.*

Disappearing Act

I read an anonymous essay online at some point in which another young woman recalled the day her brother disappeared. The facts in evidence were scant: he went camping by a lake with friends. One morning, their canoe and her brother were gone.

In chilly March weather, at night, while everyone else was asleep, presumably he decided to go canoeing by himself, which is kind of weird, but not inconceivable, and what other conclusion could they come to? After a weeks-long search, police told this woman and her family that he must have become hypothermic and drowned because all that was ever found was the canoe, partially submerged in the lake.

Suspected dead.

Even after dragging the lake, sending in scuba divers, combing the surrounding woods, and using radar detection devices, there was no body. Nobody.

I don't know how big this lake was, but I was astonished to realize this brother, or any person could simply vanish in it. I am devastated for her. Not only because it's so painful to lose a sibling, not just because it's agonizing to come to terms with a sudden death. As brutal as I know it is to lose a brother in the wilderness, *to* the wilderness—a feeling as terrifying and heart-breaking as anything I've experienced—the *not knowing* surely adds an extra layer of pure horror.

Just lost. Out there. Never found.

I don't believe in the notion of closure exactly because I've realized loss never truly ends. But never being able to find out where this man ended up or how he died or *if* he really died—instead of running away with his lover or being abducted by a lunatic or an alien spaceship—sounds to me like a recipe for madness.

And that's where her story went. She went crazy breaking things, with violence: relationships, car windows, doors, a motorcycle. She ultimately threw someone through a window and ended up in a courtroom. Surely, temporary insanity should be applied in her case. I could be a character reference, and I don't even know her.

How would her guessing, supposing, imagining, fearing, dreading ever end? I imagine it doesn't.

I didn't see my brother's body, which is at the same time relieving and dispiriting. I wouldn't necessarily want to have seen him dead, but there is a good reason open coffins exist. As unpleasant as I've found them at the few funerals I've attended where that custom was practiced, at least I could swear in a court of law that the people who once inhabited those bodies were indeed expired.

Because I saw them with my own eyes.

I didn't see my brother's body, but I trust those who did. I trust the search and rescue guys who found him, but even more, I trust his friends who were there waiting at the base of the mountain in Colorado when he was ferried down. And, in this, I trust my mother, who had the weighty obligation of identifying him in the coroner's office.

I didn't see my brother's body, so I couldn't stand up in a court of law and swear that I knew he was dead. But I believe all of them, so I have faith. When my brother went missing, his body was, at least, found. There was mystery over how his accident transpired—and that has been challenge enough to wrestle—but at least we all knew where he ended up. Over the years, that never felt much like a gift, but after hearing this woman's story, I recognize it as such. A small, but vital, one. I never knew it before, but *officially* dead is sometimes better than the alternative.

After years of binge-watching TV shows like *Without a Trace* and digging deeply into the part of my brother's story that never made sense—how someone so methodical, so heartily athletic, so experienced in the wild could end up slipping and falling from a peak he had carefully planned to summit—it never occurred to me that we might never have even found him.

It never seemed like that mystery could have been a part of my life. Despite everything that *did* become part of my life that I could never have predicted, never guessed. These things happen to other people. Like this woman. A woman like me.

I wrote to her thanking her for sharing her story, congratulating her on her bravery in the telling, offering my condolences—and that while I related to so much in her piece, I really felt for her about the part I didn't. *I can't fathom ...* I told her.

What if they never found my brother either?

What if, among the vast mountain range in Colorado, he slipped into a gully, under a fallen tree, behind a boulder? There are so many places in nature one can get lost. We only waited one day to find out David had died, and it was excruciating. What if after days and weeks of hand wringing and trying in vain to sleep at night, we were told he was only *suspected* dead? What if we had no explanation for friends and family? The conversations were so difficult as it was, and full of annoying, well-meaning platitudes: "Well, at least he was doing what he loved ..."

What if there was no body to bury or cremate, no conclusion for an obituary? How do you hold a service for someone who is simply gone?

There is little peace to be found in losing a brother, especially overnight, especially when he is healthy and vibrant, especially when he was simply enjoying Mother Nature. It is hard work under any circumstance to reconcile this as part of your story. But for the tale to be left open-ended, no final chapter, unresolved, is inconceivable to me.

It's hard enough to tell people about David's death. How would I tell them that one day he was here, and the next, he just was not?

What's Left

When David died, he was unmarried and childless (or "child-free," as he likely would have framed it). He had spent his adult life working long hours as a radiologist in part because he loved science and helping people, but in equal part because the associated paycheck and vacation time afforded him the life he really wanted. He had traveled and had many girlfriends but never yearned for a traditional family life, to the disappointment of said girlfriends. When David died, he left behind a sizable bank account, a largely unlived-in house, and a small orange tabby cat named Sam.

Once upon a time, David had had a dog, a black lab called Harley, who was genuinely his best friend and a regular companion on local journeys. Harley hung himself on his own leash by jumping out of the bed of my brother's pick-up truck where David had tethered him while he hiked nearby, and died. After that accident, David never wanted another dog. He probably didn't even want a cat, but one of those girlfriends had picked up a teensy, flea-covered stray and convinced him to keep it. Despite his resistance to the vulnerabilities of love, he fell hard for Sam.

My six-foot-tall, rugged big brother would cry out girlishly, "Squeaky! Squeaky!" to summon Sam when he got home from work. The nickname came from Sam's high-pitched voice. David would scoop him up and kiss his head and scruff loudly, unabashed. Because he often left Sam behind for extended periods when he traveled, I've always wondered how long it must have taken for Sam to realize he wasn't coming back that last time.

It took months to figure out what to do with the abandoned kitty, not because he wasn't wanted, but because my mother and I both wanted him so desperately. She and I are nearly equal crazy cat ladies. We were also equally in love with my brother and devastated by the loss. But in the end, she won out by convincing me that a plane trip to my house would traumatize Sam more than a car ride to hers.

Eight years later, Mom called me and said that Sam was barely breathing. "Do you think I've paralyzed him?" she asked, desperation in her voice as she described his condition over the phone. She had given him twice as much pain medication as prescribed after he suffered a long bout with lymphoma, willing him to die at home rather than at the vet's office.

She got her wish. A text message confirmed the little orange cat left his body that night: *I'm feeling sad ...* For me, saying goodbye to Squeaky was saying one more goodbye to my brother. I wondered if there was any shred to hold onto.

#NationalSiblingsDay

Since when did everything have a "day"? I blame social media for ensuring that not just regular birthdays, death anniversaries, and every other family-oriented holiday on the calendar, but even *more* days of the year, now pain me.

Even though I have Tommy and it's good to be reminded to appreciate him, I spend an inordinate amount of time thinking about losing David, and sometimes I want a break. Then it's April 10, #NationalSiblingsDay, which is another moment to be annoyed, if not downright weepy, while scrolling through social media channels.

One might say, "Well, just don't be online that day then!" Except I work in marketing communications, the word "digital" is in my professional job description, and social media is part of my everyday job requirement. So, there's that.

Because I'm a glutton for punishment, when I found out about this "holiday," I did some quick Google research, which told me that National Siblings Day was created by a sister just like me, who created the holiday in memory of her deceased brother—and sister. Claudia Evart had an entirely sweet idea when she conceived of the day in 1997 as an addition to Mother's Day, Father's Day, and so forth: celebrate and recognize the relationship between brothers and sisters.

I'm all over that. However, Wikipedia suggests:

Examples of commemoration during this observance include giving your sibling a gift (including a surprise gift), a gift card, and taking one out for dinner. Nonmaterial examples of observances during this day includes giving hugs to your sibling(s), enjoying time with them, and honoring their presence in your life.

Now that's just cruel when your siblings are dead. Plus, Evart chose the date specifically because it was her deceased sister's birthday. So maybe a few other suggestions are needed? Here are a few of mine:

If you're missing your brother or sister, remember how they used to pin you down, sit on your skull, and fart right into your face. Mad at them? Post a photo of them on social media from when they turned fourteen and had braces, glasses, and a bowl cut. Or decide it's okay to be a little sad, a bit melancholy, or even just quiet about it. Alternately, rant about how this is A DAY.

While National Siblings Day isn't nationally recognized, that doesn't seem to matter in the magical online worlds of Facebook, Twitter, and Instagram. I scrolled past dozens of pictures and stories and love notes and beefs written by friends and family to and about their brothers and sisters, feeling jealous, angry, sad, and invisible.

Virtual Life Goes On

Though my obsession had diminished, it hadn't gone away. Back to the online research, I Googled David's name to check in. It had been nine years, and it seemed that no results whatsoever were for him. What felt like a short amount of time to me was an eternity for the search engine algorithms. I found so many other men sporting his name: an artist, a cinematographer, a singer of a Danish/American alternative rock band, a lawyer, several professors, and, interestingly, several doctors. A barber, a real estate agent, a development director, a basketball coach. All of them feel like frauds using my brother's name.

The novelty discovery was a "David Boyd Room" in an inn, listed as "one of our most popular rooms and will be your home away from home while staying with us ..."

I kept searching, page after page, clicking Google's little blue forward arrow again and again, thinking something must have lasted; *my* David Boyd must be in here somewhere. I found a Twitter profile, an Instagram account, a number of Facebook pages. LinkedIn had 1,132 professionals named David Boyd. Where was he among these zillions of imposters?

I even tried "David Boyd athlete," and there were lots of results, so many results, none of them his. The 14ers.com site had removed the old posts.

Then I tried "David Boyd radiologist," and though I was surprised to find a number of other radiologists also bearing his name, I finally got a hit on my brother's obituary from the *Houston Chronicle* along with one tiny, unexpected treasure—his practice still had him on their website in the staff list. Clicking it directed me to a special "In Memoriam" page. At the top was a photo of him not from his work in the hospital, but from a trip MOAT took to Australia. In it, he wears a navy-blue t-shirt and dark shorts, sneakers, and a baseball cap that shades his face from the sun. On his left wrist, as always, he wears a multifunctional, chunky wristwatch. But you almost don't notice any of that since he is standing atop a small rock turret, just large enough for one person, that seems to be jutting into the frame from nowhere. Behind him span great swaths of deep green, tan coastlines, and blue bodies of water that recede into the background. He is standing on top of the world.

Underneath the picture, I was reminded of his areas of specialty: Interventional Radiology, Body Imaging, and Image Guided Biopsy, terms I would have had him define for me back in the day, but which I can't easily parse now. They list his education, his certifications, his professional memberships. Still, with the photo at the top, his radiology group allowed his athletic and outdoor passions to dominate the page and have his medical credentials take second place.

Then I found that "David Boyd adventure race" was the jackpot search phrase. Phew. Terra Firma Racing still listed him and Patti as 2007 co-ed Texas State Champions and him and his friend Wooch as the 2000 male champs. I saw that other teammates of his won those titles in the years since. There was a David Boyd Memorial Fund for the BikeTexas KidsKup. The Texas Mountain Bike Racing Association renamed their Huntsville

Classic race for him. There was now a Dave Boyd Adventure Race too. And the United States Adventure Racing Association created a Dave Boyd Spirit Award.

It's a tiny fraction of what used to be alive online, but it's reassuring that something remains, especially such good tributes.

Bad Math

March 13, 2017: David would have been fifty-six. A photo of us, my head resting on his right shoulder and Tommy sitting at his left, pops up in my Facebook feed as a "memory"—as if I would forget his birthday without this visual reminder. The photo was taken in a restaurant in Houston called Julia's where we had a fantastic dinner years ago, a restaurant that, like my brother, is now gone.

In my inbox, a daily email from the Writer's Almanac says today, March 13, is the birthday of Percival Lowell, Janet Flanner, Pope Innocent XII, even Uncle Sam—at least the day he was "born" in the form of a cartoon character in 1852 in a publication called the *New York Lantern*. It seems David's name, far more important to me than any of these, should also appear here in the list of VIP birthdays as I scroll.

Wikipedia says, "March 13 is the 72nd day of the year (73rd in leap years) in the Gregorian calendar. There are 293 days remaining until the end of the year." There are 365 days—or 364 if next year is a leap year—before I feel quite this feeling again.

I had seen Tommy in person the week before in Houston, when he turned fifty-three. I knew the proximity in their birthdays brought both celebration and competition growing up. Now it causes only sadness. Already, Tommy's lifespan has surpassed David's by six years, which seems like bad math; David was born three years before Tommy. But this is what death does; it changes calculations. It made Tommy not just my only, but also my oldest, brother.

Forty-seven years isn't so bad in terms of duration, and anyone who knew David knew that he lived more than most people do in a lifetime in his four and a half decades. Still, it's hard not to feel cheated each and every year, as I am greedy. Wanting so much more.

You can't add to a life story post death.

Though I did have a new dream about David, a phenomenon so rare it might have been only the third time he appeared in my unconsciousness this way, unsummoned by me, a welcome visitor. In the scene, David was driving a speedboat—too fast, no surprise—while I sat in the seat behind him, being splashed with spray and laughing raucously. It felt dangerous and safe at the same time, a sense my brother provoked easily. Upon waking, I cried as I had cried when I lost him in real life, the way waking up reminded me of the reality each and every day for years, and not just on his birthday.

It was strange, as always, to be back "home" in Houston, surrounded in our mother's house by her photos and mementos of David—her own shrine, different from mine—reminding me of our deeply varied relationships, the relationships that still "go on and on" for each of us, even now, as the wise writer Kim Stafford, who also lost a brother, recently wrote me.

I have not yet lived as long as David did, but I hope to, and I hope to surpass him too, as weird as that will be. As the baby of the family, I wonder if I will outlive everyone eventually, if not also go beyond their years, their numbers, their experiences. I wonder, as many of us must do, whether we will meet again, somewhere where numbers don't exist.

Further Investigation

An essay I wrote about David was published online, and I shared it on my Facebook page and Twitter feed, excited for the credit and nervous about its contents. Though I didn't realize it until dozens of comments poured in, it was the first time many of my friends found out I was writing about my brother, and it was the first announcement to some that I had even lost him. Still others who had gleaned that David was dead didn't know how it had happened.

Beyond my extreme gratitude for the exposure to his story and a validation of my writing, I was stunned and humbled by the reaction from friends and acquaintances, many of whom commented specifically on parts they loved or gave me incredible reassurances overall as both a human and an author. It meant a great deal to connect with people in this way, especially over what was arguably the biggest event of my life, and one that had been so deeply isolating.

But the message that took my breath away was one I received in private from John, David's stepbrother, Sarah's son. I had met him only once, in Houston at the memorial service. He wrote to me, mysteriously: *I read your piece and I have information you might want.*

I remembered that John had been involved in some way when David went missing, but never really understood the scope. He and I connected by phone the following Saturday.

"I have a sort of report I put together at the time if you want me to send it to you," he said. Yes, of course, I wanted the report. "I would have sent it ahead of time, but it seemed like it might be better to walk you through it.

"It seems like you still haven't found any closure yet," he went on. Surely meaning it kindly, it still smarted. After nine years, I learned there wasn't any such thing as closure, but he was right that I hadn't been able to put this story to bed, so I didn't respond.

John emailed an eighteen-page PDF, text with a lot of inserted graphics, which I opened on my laptop while cradling the phone between my shoulder and ear. The main focus at the beginning of the document was tracking David's final movements, part of John's own quest to understand what might have happened. Three photos showed our brother's handwriting on the ledgers from his three final peaks; proof positive that he had summited. Though he had a doctor's classical scribbly signature, David's regular handwriting had always been very clear, and his brief notes on each of the logbook photos were easily legible: on Blanca, he had written, *Cool place*; on Ellingwood, *Hammer Time* ...; on Little Bear, again, *3rd Peak Today! Nice & Dry*.

The excitement of that last one. I flinched seeing it, despite already knowing it existed. I flinched knowing these lines had become investigative clues. I flinched knowing they were the final artifacts from his life.

A chart on a map plotted thirty-nine "tracks," dots for each signal reported from the SPOT locator, including times plus latitude and longitude points. The marks confirmed the time David reached the top of Little Bear—2:49 p.m.—and the time shortly after when we assume he fell. What had troubled John the most was the fact that the SPOT tracker sent out signals after that—seven times, in fact—into the following day. That made John worry that David had either been hurt and *then* fallen, or worse, that he might have tried to use the SPOT to call for help *after* falling since the final dots moved around a bit.

"You're kidding!" I blurted, trying not to cry. I had never known there was a chance that David had been suffering on the mountainside. It was too much to consider. Yet we did.

A news story, which I gratefully hadn't read at the time, published in a local Alamosa paper three days after David's body was found, reinforced this appalling possibility: "A SPOT tracker was able to aid rescuers in the location of a missing hiker in the Sangre de Cristos mountains, but a distress signal from the man's positioning transmitter was not received in time by local authorities to save his life."

Naturally, John had been extremely alarmed by that possibility. I was alarmed nine years later, having always been told, and believed, that death was instantaneous.

"It appeared that Boyd fell 150-200 feet and succumbed to his injuries in the hours that passed after he activated this GPS unit's emergency option … The article continued. The victim may have moved only a few feet from when the signal was originally sent at 9:18 p.m."

This was downright nauseating, conjuring an image of our dear brother, a doctor, in mortal agony, crawling on the ground for hours, desperate for help that wouldn't arrive in time. Even the reference to him as a "victim" was off-putting.

A long gap between time markers at the end was especially bizarre; all of the previous lapses were only ten minutes or so. The 9:18 p.m. mark was more than six hours after the fall. John had called and talked to the SPOT company several times and learned that the device relies on GPS satellite constellation just like any navigation system and needs to "see" the sky through a single antenna on the front of the device. Densely forested areas and high mountains meant fixes were sometimes lost or inaccurate. Combined with the fact that Kevin Wright, the head of the SAR team, told John the SPOT beacon was found twenty feet downhill from David's body, face down on the side of a slope, could explain the erratic communication.

It still wasn't enough for John to have complete peace of mind, which I entirely understood, despite the fact that it wouldn't have changed anything. Wright also told John that where he might have expected blood from lacerations on David's body, there wasn't much, speculating that was "due to lack of heart function." Right. You can't bleed if your heart is stopped. Suddenly things were very medical, very bodily instead of technical. Medical in a way that I used to pick up the phone to ask David about. Attempting to make sense of it without him, about him, really burned.

Wait. Way back when she identified the body, hadn't Mom said he *was* bloody? I didn't say this out loud to John. It was all so newly confusing.

His conversations with the coroner who performed the autopsy and the chief coroner of Colorado Springs took place on the next pages. There had been an ankle injury, which I completely forgot about, but that Mom definitely had mentioned. Could it have happened prior to the fall? Some swelling and hemorrhaging suggested it could have. *Might he have hurt his ankle, attempted to get off the ridge, and then fallen? Might he have hurt his ankle in the process of falling?* John wondered on the page.

He asked the coroner about the lack of blood at the scene, adding that it had rained that night, which might have washed it away. Might David have been alive, but unconscious, due to his head wounds?

I didn't know there were head wounds. Mom specifically told me that the helmet had kept his head intact.

With all the information John was able to share after talking to the SAR team and researching the functionality of the SPOT locator, plus a conversation with the local sheriff and deputy, they came to the conclusion that David's injuries all happened at the same time. He would have immediately lost consciousness when he hit his head, and John wrote, *The heart injury would have resulted in immediate loss of blood to the brain, with death taking place in as little as second, certainly not more than a minute.*

Oof, a phrase like, "the heart injury." It was all kinds of symbolic. I was actively weeping then, but quietly. I hoped John couldn't tell.

Pages in the document were dedicated to additional conversations and email communications he had had with hikers who were on the trail that day, as well as posts from the fourteeners website. To understand what might have provoked the fall, they discussed at length the storm that rolled in that afternoon. More than one had been concerned about clouds and fog. Another confirmed there had been rain and hail late in the day, but others who had actually met David on Ellingwood just before his accident said the thunder and lightning didn't start until closer to 5 p.m.

A commenter in the document named Scott Thomas, who was on the mountain that day wrote, "I can say confidently that weather was not a direct cause of David's fall ... David would have had a very clear view of this weather moving in, and he would have been able to see that it was electrical and known that he needed to get down in a hurry … He may have started moving a bit too fast (his normal pace was already blinding) and taken a bad step. Or he may have chosen to take the steeper, more dangerous couloir in which he fell in order to get down faster. Or he may have taken it inadvertently, thinking it was the correct descent. I guess we'll never know for sure."

Right. That is the hard part.

Was it weird that I was also still proud of my brother's "blinding" pace?

At least three groups of hikers reported hearing "an incredibly loud rockslide" around 3 p.m. and saw dust clouds rise on Little Bear's west ridge. Nobody signed the log after David that day.

Though the talk with John opened up distressing questions I had never had, he largely solved them for me within half an hour and reaffirmed that there are certain parts of that last day we will never be sure about. It pained me to know John had stomached so much thinking about the possibility that our beloved brother had been mortally wounded, in excruciating pain, and alone.

But our conversation made *me* feel less crazy and alone in needing answers after our terrible loss. Here was someone else in the family who was not only willing but also driven to dig into the situation, ugly and painful as it was. I felt freakishly bonded to him in thirty minutes, and I was grateful for the connection.

John's final steps were literal. The following summer, Wright and another of the search and rescue guys who found David led John all the way up Little Bear to the final spot.

"I'm taking Peyton there in September," I told him, "I mean, to Alamosa, not all the way up to that spot. Unless you think I could make it?"

"By the end, I was huffing and puffing behind those guys," he said, "but you could do it."

I wondered.

John said he still had a few of David's bikes, and he rode them all the time. "You're in better shape than I am, for sure," I said, "but I'll think about it."

Signing off the call, John told me, "It feels good to talk about him. I haven't thought about this in a long time."

Me, always the little sister, always missing my big brother, replied, "Well, you're practically my brother too. Any time you want to talk."

"Thanks. I'm going to go take a bike ride now," he finished, and in his voice, I heard the same happy bounce I remembered in David's voice when he was about to head out.

Tribute to the Mountains

Because I'd spent so much time reading about David through the online fourteeners community, I grew affection for the commenters—the many strangers who said such nice things about him—and though it seems ironic, over time, I grew affectionate toward those 14,000-foot mountains themselves: for the adventure, perspective, and sense of achievement they offer those who managed their way up the steep, scree-strewn, treacherous slopes. For my own love of nature, how it is my true church, how much it was also David's. And even for how the fourteeners are a truly beautiful place to die.

Though there were Texas groups that started funds in David's memory for kids' biking and there were races named after him—places that friends and family directed well-wishers who wanted to make charitable contributions in my brother's honor—it was the Colorado Fourteeners Initiative that I focused on from the very beginning.

CFI constructs and maintains the vast network of trails throughout the mountains that hikers travel up and down peaks throughout the state. Their mission also appeals to my environmental interests, as the group strives to preserve wild habitats and ecosystems despite the throngs of visitors and encourages "Leave

No Trace" habits. Almost exclusively, volunteers conduct their work. Most of all, I was sold on their commitment to educating guests on mountain safety. I suppose, though it wasn't at all clear to me the first year I sent them a donation (was anything clear to me that first year?), I felt I was supporting another adventurer's safe passage; that I was contributing to an effort that might, in some way, assure that someone else's beloved friend, teammate, son, or brother came home.

Today, the CFI annual report came in the mail, a yearly package that, as a marketer, I love for its beautiful design and photography, great storytelling and infographics, and a piece I used to look forward to because I could turn to the back and see David's name in print, my gift in his honor. It was wonderful news that the organization was now too big to name small donors like me; since my brother's fall, their assets have multiplied eight times. That year, I was anonymously lumped into a number: 516 "Supporting Donors," those of us who gave $50. My few dollars have helped fill their bucket for the last decade, and at least I still get to type David's name on the "in memory", line on the online donation form each year, and maybe someone still reads it.

The executive director writes compelling appeal letters, one year even throwing in a line like, *you are helping the mountains David loved* ... and I wondered whether that was just from some automatic merge field in their database or whether he actually saw my brother's name and knew the story, or at least wondered. Regardless, it was effective.

This year the brochure's cover features a colorful, panoramic spread of the mountains looking very much like I remember them: above the tree line, the rocky crests are scrubbed bare by severe cold, wind, and weather; below, their sloping sides are peppered with dark pines that thicken densely at lower elevation and eventually merge with bright golden patches I now recognize as stands of aspen trees exploding with fall color near the bottom. I never knew I could look at a landscape and find it equal parts terrifying and dreamily gorgeous.

For the first time, a page inside the report is dedicated to educating hikers about risk and includes a screenshot from an online *Outside* article about a record number of fatalities there last year. The text says an estimated 334,000 people traversed the fourteeners in 2017, and a six percent increase is anticipated annually. Despite the deaths, the flood of visitors shows no signs of slowing.

I need none of this to compel me, but I read it all anyway, despite the way it pains me some, then make my 2018 gift, my tenth, my ongoing tribute to those mountains.

Keepsakes

After three rounds of in vitro fertilization, my dear friend's long-ached-for infant daughter was born at five and a half months and died after just a few hours. Monica kept the tiny girl's ashes in a pretty, miniature urn on a shelf. A few years later, she came across a woman who creates "memorial jewelry" with cremains of beloved people and pets, and she had a ring made with a pinch of her baby's ashes.

Over cocktails one evening in a cozy dark bar, we bonded over what we had been doing with our respective loved ones' deaths, attempting to turn the awful into something better. She had started working with other bereaved mothers; I was writing about the loss of siblings. Both of us were trying to reach out to others like us so that they felt a little less alone. Both of us still were—and always would be—grieving what we would never have again.

Monica showed me the new ring, simple and clean, silver set with a quartz stone, under which nearly invisible traces of her most precious, hardest won thing are pressed. The ring carries a piece of her inside, a lovely secret if she wishes to keep it that way, a conversation piece if not.

More and more, she told me, she had been answering the bitterly painful question that others, unthinking, considered innocuous small talk, "Do you have kids?" with the truth instead of hiding it. "I had a baby who died. Her name was Josie." This was healthy. This was brave. I was moved and inspired by Monica's willingness to go there.

For years, I had largely answered the difficult question about whether I had siblings with, simply, "I have a brother." It always bothered me that this answer not only belies the truth (and I am a truth-teller), but also erases David from my story. It isn't convenient to bring up death when someone is attempting to break the ice, but perhaps the more we respond with something like, "I have one surviving sibling. My brother David is dead," the more we can normalize this process and honor those who impacted us so deeply.

Sitting at the bar, my sweet friend and I clinked glasses full of Old Fashioneds, toasting each other for surviving. Though it was the last thing we would have wished on each other, we were grateful to be with each other as members of the same club.

I mentioned to her that, inside a silver box engraved with his initials that I had given him for Christmas years before, I had a large quantity of David's ashes. I had kept the box on a shelf in my bedroom all these years as part of a sort of makeshift altar that also held his iPod, a Dia de los Muertos candle, an orange WWDBD bracelet, a tiny plastic statue of The Little Prince, an orienteering compass, and photographs Glenn had taken during Primal Quest, one from my wedding, and the last I had taken of him myself at a cyclocross race in Rhode Island in 2006. I had only managed to scatter a small handful of the ashes on what would have been his fiftieth birthday after a climb up the mountain behind our house.

My friend gave me contact information for the memorial jewelry lady. Within weeks, I contacted her.

She wrote me back right away: *I'm sorry you lost your brother. I'd love to make something for you. The process: The ashes have to be sent Express mail shipping through USPS. They also should have stickers that say "cremated remains" for the envelope, and the signature required box should be checked on the form. I only need a little pinch sent in a lightweight container or sealed bag inside the envelope with your name clearly written on it.*

Why would the process be any less strange than all of the handling of ashes I'd dealt with so far? Here I was, back to an unceremonial plastic baggie into which I had poured approximately a quarter of a teaspoon's worth of ashes, my name written on it in Sharpie, tucked inside a card, reading *Thank you*.

It was a little awkward telling the postal clerk about my package as I leaned over her counter; it was clearly an unusual request, as it took her a while to locate the necessary sticker. And there was no conceivable rationale for needing to have ashes shipped overnight with a signature requirement. These weren't biologically active materials, but I guess knowing that they came from a body is enough to make people edgy, and therefore, need to get it over with as quickly as possible. The large, black, unmissable sticker made certain that the package must have been weird for the carrier to deliver.

The jeweler confirmed receipt of David's ashes when they arrived and told me she would send my pendant in about eight weeks.

Above the Clouds

From time to time, I thought about Shaun and the fourteen REI tubes—the ones full of David's ashes that I had thrust into his hands—and I wondered if he'd made any other ascents, though I thought he would have told me if he had. I certainly never wanted to pressure him. I knew that in the years following David's death, Shaun and his wife had had three children and that he kept running an active construction business, plus I assumed that somewhere in the back of his mind was completely understandable fear. If he never scaled another mountain in his life, I respected that choice.

Who could blame anyone from David's team for quitting all of those exploits after such a trauma? David was a cautionary tale if ever there was one.

Leslie, so visibly shaken in the aftermath of the accident, had taken time off from all racing, and I found that perfectly under-standable too. But I couldn't help being delighted when I saw a post on her Facebook page that she had finally decided to compete in a biking tournament again. All of the MOAT crew were such expert cyclers—it was always their biggest strength in adventure races—and I knew it brought them joy to pedal.

So, I was ecstatic when I scrolled through Facebook one night in 2017 and saw that she was prepping for the Adventure Racing

World Championship in Wyoming, especially when I read this note: "Couldn't sleep much tonight in anticipation of the start … I always hoped I could still do it at age forty-seven, the age of Dave Boyd when he died. This race will be in memory of DB and Team MOAT."

Way to get back on the horse! I thought proudly, if also a little tearfully. Though I could have wanted all of them to stay grounded—to stay safe—after everything I'd learned, I finally felt I knew their kind. And their kind was only half alive without quests, without physical striving. Her team finished, and performed well, and I was thrilled for her, reclaiming her passion that way.

I couldn't have asked for more from David's teammates. But it came.

In August of 2018, just one week before Peyton and I were heading to Colorado to mark the tenth anniversary of David's fall, Shaun sent an email to Mom and me:

Good morning,

Leslie and I are headed to the top of Mt. Rainier.

We head to the base camp today and will plan to leave for the summit about 12 a.m. Thursday. We have done training the last few days with a few other peeps and we all feel pretty good. The weather looks to be great.

See you soon!

Two days later, he wrote: *We summited with Dave early Thursday a.m.*

An attached photograph showed the side of Leslie's face barely poking out under a helmet, sunglasses, and neck warmer, her arm extended over pristine blue sky and swaths of pure white clouds, god rays shot through the top edge of the frame. In her gloved hand, an open REI tube scattered ashes across what might as well have been heaven. That it wasn't a mountain in Colorado made no difference to me. It was the height that counted.

Dave got another 14er :)

Love – Shaun

Flight Risk

At last, the trip I planned in my mind for years and scheduled months ahead of time is finally happening. It's August 30, 2018, and Peyton and I are sitting on the plane on the tarmac in Hartford waiting to take off for Denver. I've been looking forward to this excursion for so long, though when I excitedly told Mom about our plans, she said only, "That sounds sad."

I'm glad it's Peyton here with me on this tenth anniversary trip. I'm joyful to be going back to beautiful southern Colorado and to share it with him. I'm pleased he'll, at last, be able to have his moment—an opportunity to honor David since he missed the memorial ten years earlier because of his tour schedule. This feels right. I feel emotional, and very moved, but not actually sad, and also freer than I have in some time.

Just the day before, I accepted a new job and tendered my resignation at my current one. Clipping my seat belt, I announce glibly, "I quit my job, and I'm leaving town!" though the decision hadn't been made lightly and the timing was a fluke.

"Flight risk!" he says back, and we laugh.

In interviews, I acknowledge the obvious from looking at my resume: that I've held quite a few positions in the recent past. I say it really isn't like me; there were powers out of my control, and that I am eager to find a great fit where I can "make a differ-ence for a long time." This is both true and not true. I count and realize the new job will be my seventh since David died.

"I *am* a flight risk," I confess. "It's David's fault."

His early death changed my attitude toward a lot of things and limited my patience. I absolutely can't tolerate mediocrity, inau-thenticity, or drudgery, especially at work, no matter how irre-sponsible the repercussions might seem. I've given up retirement pay, raises, vacation time, and promotion opportunities to try something else, something that might be better. The days at a job are too long, and the cliché holds that life is too short. Despite being deeply responsible and a creature of habit in many ways, I now have a hard time settling for any bullshit, which occasion-ally means I'm less reliable than I once was. The idea of spending forty hours a week doing something I hate just isn't possible long-term anymore. I want to come to the end of my own life, however brief or long, knowing I didn't settle that way.

As we take off and begin to ascend, significant turbulence starts rocking the plane, which always terrifies me. My palms start sweating when the captain asks the flight attendants to be seated and tells us to stay put, seatbelts fastened. Internally, I curse my irrational fear. I was in such a great headspace when we took off. Why is panic rising in my chest?

Peyton lets me clutch his arm and shows me videos of our dogs playing in the backyard on his iPhone to distract me. I don't have to say anything. He knows. I pop a Xanax (brought for these exact moments), cry a little, and remember David once saying of flying, "It never bothers me."

Of course, it didn't. Scientist, doctor, adventurer, risk taker. I wonder if his brain was wired differently, the way the free-soloing rock climber Alex Honnold's is, with an unresponsive amygdala, without fear, at least the way most of us experience it.

"When he's free soloing, it's when he feels the most ..." Honnold's mother says to the camera in the film, *Free Solo.* Then she pauses, and I think something else is coming: the most alive, the most excited, the most successful. "It's when he feels *the most*," she reiterates, describing her son's singular passion. "How can you take that away from someone?"

The movie documents Honnold's incredible 2017 rope-free ascent of El Capitan, a sheer vertical 3,000 foot wall in Yosemite, a physical and psychological achievement considered to be one of the most impressive in all of climbing history, but it also goes into who he is, how he was raised, why he wants/needs to do this, offering insight into the man behind the sinewy frame and cool demeanor, as well as a perspective from those who care about him: his girlfriend, his climbing partners, the film crew, his mom. "I'm glad he doesn't tell me when he free solos," she ends.

Maybe, I'm just weak. My brother was so strong! I remind myself for the thousandth time how much more dangerous driving is than flying, climbing without ropes over hiking, but it doesn't help. Nothing about this moment is rational.

I try to imagine David whispering in my ear, "It's okay, darlin'." But he isn't here.

Standing in a line of dozens of other customers snaking through stanchions at Budget Rent-a-Car, I curse David aloud for dying on a holiday weekend. It's Labor Day for everyone else, though we are observing our own strange holiday. After the stressful plane trip, I am eager to be in control of my own travel, to steer myself and Peyton the rest of the way.

When booking a car, I had remembered from my last visit to Colorado with Mom that many of the places near the Sangre de Cristo Mountains are accessible only by dirt roads, and that some of them turn into rocky roads that turn into bouldered roads, so I reserved a mid-sized SUV. Once we finally reach the service counter, the rental agent gives us the options. "Would you like a Jeep or a Subaru?"

"A Subaru," I declare for no particular reason, just impatient to go.

"Okay," he says. "Go out to row E, number 20."

In an enormous lot, bigger than most car dealerships I've seen, and jammed with vehicles of all shapes, sizes, and colors, Peyton and I amble through a backwards alphabet: J, I, H, G, F, E, turn right and count forwards 17, 18, 19, 20. I gasp and then laugh out loud when I see the Subaru Cross Trek that we are about to set out in. It is brilliant orange.

The car is the identical color of David's infamous last bike. It appears the same hue as the WWDBD bracelets his team-mates handed out at the memorial service. I specifically had that shade of orange tattooed onto the belly of the bird on my back. The Sangre de Cristos (meaning Blood of Christ) are named such because of the reddish orange they reflect at sunrise and sunset. At moments like this, it's easy to think everything is a sign, but if there was a signature color for David's death, it was this unapologetically vibrant orange.

Orange, a complimentary color, composed of red for energy and yellow for happiness. I love it. It makes me downright giddy to jump into this car.

Maybe he is here after all.

Weather Phenomena

The sky expresses multiple personalities from the moment we leave Denver and start driving south. Looking left, a hazy gray curtain of rain veils colossal mountain ranges. In the opposite direction, puffy clouds brightly reflect honey-colored sunshine. In front of us, a sharp bolt of lightning cuts through the sky vertically, stabbing the horizon. Later, a greenish hue paints our view—"tornado sky," I learned from growing up in Texas—and I worry we are witnessing small funnels attempting to form.

It's a four-and-a-half-hour drive to Alamosa. The topography doesn't change much, but clouds shift from luminous streaks to bright dapples to ungainly blobs with dark shadowy underbellies. Pale, washed-out blue sky behind them deepens to azure and then drains to a soft gray. The light transforms the peaks in the distance into charcoal smudges, then dull brown crags, and finally, looking out, I consider how the phrase "purple mountains majesty" must have been inspired.

The one-room cabin we rented in Alamosa, just seven miles from Little Bear, offers a perfect view of the peaks. After dinner that first night, Peyton and I go outside behind the cabin with a joint and a beer.

"Wow!" I say, looking up for the first time since darkness set in. What I first thought was a ridge of clouds because of its pale density, reveals itself as the Milky Way, its billions of constellations parading across the sky. It has been so long since I've had an unimpeded view of stars, and they seem shinier than usual, extra twinkly, sparkling clean.

"And over there, it looks like Vietnam," Peyton says, pointing north, I think. And it really does look like ground combat is taking place over a ridge; lighting explodes through the dark in yellow bursts, but it is absolutely soundless where we are. No thunder at all. Just eerie quiet with intermittent flashes of light. Low sets of clouds glow, as if from within, gold and black, there and gone, behind—or over—or above? Silhouettes of mountains. The landscape is so wide, it seems immeasurable. The lights are far off, I'm not sure exactly what I'm seeing, and all of it is too far away to hear.

When we don't talk, it is the quietest place I've ever been. The only sound is from the lip of my beer bottle singing in the wind.

Why does so much weather happen around the memory of my brother? Am I trying to make mystical what is just nature being its amazing self?

I look up and see not one, but three, shooting stars.

We hear a bark in the distance. "A coyote," Peyton says. I argue it must be a dog, but soon a group joins voices in a sad chorus. The coyotes cry all night long, their baying an echo of my long internal wail.

Things in the Distance
Are Farther Away
Than They Appear

"Will I ever be able to look at that mountain without crying?"
I say to Peyton as my eyes well at the view of the Sangre de
Cristos. I'm eyeing it from the wildlife refuge the following day,
and it seems both quite close and far away at the same time. As if
to buoy my spirits, two young elk surprise us, bounding happily
through the cattails next to us.

Perspective is warped. I can't trust my normal sense of scale.
The straight, flat road east from the cabin toward the mountain
seems to take forever, though it does loom even larger every few
minutes.

In the Great Sand Dunes National Park, we walk and walk and
walk some more through the sand. So bizarre to find this beach
in the mountains, and the dune in front of us, toward which we
are aiming, seems unreachable. The visitors on top, or sliding
down the slopes on boards, look like ants on an anthill. Back in
the car, we drive past a sign that ominously reads, "Point of no
return," a spot in any other setting where I would turn around,
but my spirit of adventure is alight. We end up where we seem

face to face with a dune, but it is so massive, it dwarfs the microscopic figures scaling it. They look like dots with arms and legs instead of full-scale humans. .

Through "wetlands" we stumble upon, several small lakes have been dried to their cores, white minerals coating their surfaces bright as snow. Red plants grow in the salt like some kind of seaweed that has learned to breathe oxygen. Charcoal dark clouds roll in, the wind whips our hair, and as we turn to leave, an enormous flock of birds I recognize from their red caps as sandhill cranes, flies by, a line of them perfectly parallel to the ground. Aren't they out of season?

The San Luis Valley has a landscape like grief: just as you think you know where you are, have oriented yourself to the landscape, the light shifts. Familiar yet always changing, colors soften or brighten, a dark bank of new clouds masks the mountain range.

I drive us to Zapata Falls, a waterfall embedded in the side of the mountains, and the guidebook isn't exaggerating calling it *rough road*; it's the roughest I've handled, with many switchbacks. The orange Subaru manages, bumping along violently, though Peyton confesses later he had been a little worried. *But I guess she's going for it!*

From the parking lot alone, the view is amazing: the sweeping sand dunes, the jagged side of the mountain range. Low pines, juniper, sage, paddle cactus, and small yellow flowers grow despite popping through barren-looking cracked brown earth. It has been an extra dry season, and still these hardy plants grow.

Up a half-mile path, the sound of white noise increases until we reach a creek bed, and cold air rushes over us like a ghost.

Peyton, his foot sore, waits for me. I tiptoe over the rocks in the stream, which is the only pathway, and I am nimble enough my shoes never get wet. Having looked at my feet the entire way, I am caught off guard when I turn into a thin opening in the cliff wall and look up. Despite the drought, the falls cascade deafeningly in front of me, splashing onto the rocks below, and I am wedged deep inside the mountain, all by myself. My hand on the freezing wall to steady myself, I look upward through a broken seam and see the sky. Adrenaline rushes through me even as I feel such peace, the chilly spray baptizing my face.

I want to linger, but soon a father and his young son wade into my haven, and I remember Peyton is waiting on the other side.

Full Circle

September 3, 2018: ten full years without David. And, also, ten years more *with* him than ever before.

Late morning, we leave the security of our snug log cabin and go in search of Little Bear. Thick, gray clouds gather overhead. Me, always heading right into a storm. But in this tough orange car, I feel oddly protected. Peyton is in the passenger seat, and I steer us, not entirely confident about where we're going, but trusting we'll find it. As we point toward the Sangre de Cristos, the sky continues to darken, inky and somber. I feel sure that as we drive higher and begin to hike, the rain, missing all summer, is bound to come in earnest, a deluge. I'm annoyed, but undeterred.

We drive and drive some more, the mountain seeming to recede rather than come closer, this land with its illusions again disorienting me. How can seven miles seem so far away? Finally, we turn right, our small vessel flanked against the side of the imposing behemoths, which I side-eye for a few miles until the range begins to slope downward, as if becoming gentler, making an offering. We take a left off the main road and creep along down familiar lonely dirt roads, treeless, vulnerably open to the sky, toward what I am pretty sure is Little Bear. Again, as we bump and lurch over larger and larger rocks, Colorado proves there is no such thing as a truly all-terrain vehicle. We ditch the Subaru among some scrub pines and sage brush to hike.

I recognize the path from the visit nine years before with Mom; it was both the same and different. Anyway, I was different. I am different.

I recognize the feel of the dusty ground under my sneakers, uneven, slippery in a way. I recognize the tiny cacti thrusting their tiny quills. I recognize the evergreen trees higher up on the mountain, so deeply green as to appear black in the shadows. I recognize the aspens, their heart-shaped leaves turning gold. I recognize the sense of not being sure what to do, what I expect of this moment, what I will get from being here.

We aren't fit enough to go terribly far, which is a minor disappointment to me, having had irrational fantasies of climbing the whole thing, but with just a bit of effort, Peyton and I reach a high spot that provides an excellent view both straight up the mountain and down it, across the sweeping San Luis Valley below, an enormous bowl made of peaks on all sides. I pretend we have made it to some halfway point, though I know that isn't true. It's probably more like a hundredth of the way up, but I like where we have arrived. Just as we decide to stop, sunshine breaks through the clouds, downright majestic.

Peyton brought the good idea to build a cairn. He also encouraged me, in preparation for this moment, to bring the rest of David's ashes, the ones that had been tucked away in that silver box for a decade. The ones I had kept just a pinch of for my keepsake necklace. The ones I always meant to scatter in wild places just like this but had barely begun to do. I had clutched them so tightly for so long, as if letting go of them would mean letting go of David, leaving him behind somewhere. It was time, he felt, for a symbolic release.

The ashes had weighed heavily on me every day we had been in Colorado. I'd carried the parcel with me in my pack during the trip, eyeing them from time to time, and I wasn't sure I'd be able to let them go.

Between the peak and the valley, on the lower slope of Little Bear, we begin to build, selecting stones with care. Stones the size of grapefruits, cantaloupes, small watermelons. We position them thoughtfully off to the side of the path below a low ledge so as not to interfere with travelers and, hopefully, to withstand weather, at least for a while. Under the now beaming sun, I peel off layers of clothing, begin to sweat. Considering the stability and architecture of our structure, we stack and nestle rocks until the pile is a stable triangular shape, perhaps three feet high. Standing back, we review and approve of our work.

I can't help but notice that the dirt on the incline there is *like* ashes, the texture so similar: uneven, full of fragments, toothy. I know my brother—all that is left of him—will become invisible, mixed in, integrated, hidden. The whole *ashes to ashes, dust to dust* thing finally makes concrete sense. The moment has arrived, and I have arrived, at last, to meet it.

Not talking, I open the baggie of ashes and pour about a third of them into Peyton's cupped palms. Reverently, but not sentimentally, he opens his hands over the cairn, and I watch the small cloud dissipate, nearly microscopic traces of the body David once inhabited easily disappear into the rocks. In turn, with my right hand, I pour half of what remains into my left hand, and, following Peyton's lead, I scatter its contents over the cairn.

I turn to give him more, and he looks me in the eye and says, "Those ones are just for you."

I take a sharp breath.

Then I do an about face, turning away from him. I hike a bit higher, until I am just out of sight behind a boulder, alone. It is almost silent, just the sound of the breeze riffling a few leaves. In private, I let the last of the ashes spill into my open hand. I close my fingers and close my eyes, feeling the way my brother's body had long ago already changed back to this substance so much like earth. Through tears, I watch the gray figments fly against the pure blue as I toss them skyward. My body sighs. I am awash with relief. I stare up at Little Bear, holding the peak in my gaze for a few seconds, and say, "Okay. He's yours."

It is both hard and right to give my brother back to nature. We, who have carried him for so many years, have all been handing him back over time, fistful by fistful, spreading his life, his zeal, his lessons across the country, the globe.

For a long time, Peyton and I sit on rocks in the path, looking out, basking in the sun. I can't figure out what direction we're facing, as usual, but I'm okay with it. The quiet between us is comfortable. I feel more relaxed than I have in a long time.

After a while, he says, "It was nice of David to die in such a beautiful place."

"Yeah," I chuckle. "We would never be here otherwise."

"So, that's a gift."

I thank David for dying in such a magnificent spot, challenging though it is to locate in its remoteness. Going there to honor him required a sense of adventure on our part—something he, in his intense drive to experience as much of nature's beauty as possible, would have appreciated. We would never have seen this exquisite piece of the world if it were not for his death there. We would never have fallen in love with it.

Without all the studying and questioning, I wouldn't be standing here thinking: wouldn't it be something to even feel a tiny bit of greatness, if not, actually, *the most*?

I would never have asked for any of this, yet my life is better for it.

In processing the loss of my beloved brother, I've always moved toward the grief rather than away from it—even afraid, I keep going, in awe of its largess, not unlike a 14,000-foot mountain. Allowing it room in my life despite the space it takes up, honoring it for what it has taught me, owning the way it changed me, making peace with it, accepting that the grief isn't going away.

I can't believe I've lived for a whole decade without David. I can't believe I've survived. I can't believe I'm stronger—physically and in every other way—than I was before. It's challenging to reconcile that the biggest loss in my life brought about the biggest rewards.

It's especially odd to realize that, above all, I am so much closer to my brother now than I ever was when he was alive. That somehow he is with me—and will always be—in ways he might not have had he lived.

So, yes, I can answer definitively now. We are very, very close.

"It is not the mountains we conquer, but ourselves."
Sir Edmund Hillary

Acknowledgements

It takes a proverbial village to launch a book into the world. This village helped me not just survive my loss, but turn it into something new:

Big thanks to Peyton Pinkerton, who lived with me through many of these experiences, as well as the drafting of this book. He helped with gaps in my grief-riddled memory and served as an avid reader and champion for this story.

I'll forever be grateful to my Bay Path University MFA writing community—enduring advisers, confidants, cheerleaders, and friends. Special appreciation for Leanna James Blackwell, Suzanne Strempek Shea, Kate Whouley, Tommy Shea, and Mel Allen, without whom I might never have had the confidence to share a word of this.

Love to Becky Miller, who was the first to open me up to this hard, vital work.

Thank you, Straw Dog Writers Guild and Patricia Lee Lewis, who provided essential community and facilitated the writing retreat at Patchwork Farm that provided me the solitude and space to complete the manuscript that became this book.

Big shoutout to Silver Jews, especially Cassie Berman, for all the affection, understanding, and support—and for the music. Always the music.

Gratitude to the team members of MOAT, especially Shaun Bain, Leslie Reuter, and Patti Plagman, who spent time illuminating the world of adventure racing for me and describing who my brother was on the road and on the course.

Great appreciation to mountaineer/author/search and rescue worker Mark Scott-Nash for allowing me to reprint lines from his book, *Colorado 14er Disasters*, and for letting me grill him with questions about adventure and risk.

Thanks to photographer Glennon Simmons for documenting MOAT's Primal Quest race and graciously sharing amazing images with me.

I am wildly grateful for the few other authors tackling the subject of sibling loss. Books that particularly mattered when I was doing this work include *The Empty Room* by Elizabeth Davita-Raeburn, *Surviving the Death of a Sibling* by T. J. Wray, *History of a Suicide* by Jill Bialosky, *Invisible Sisters* by Jessica Handler, *The Blessing* by Gregory Orr, *Barefoot to Avalon* by David Payne, *Name All the Animals* by Alison Smith, and *100 Tricks Every Boy Can Do* by Kim Stafford.

I am also thankful for the 14ers.com group and the Colorado Fourteeners Initiative for the communities they foster and the wisdom they share.

Thanks to my family and would-be-family members, who share my lasting love, sadness, and wondering, and who contributed to this story: Judy Viebig, Richard Viebig, Tom Boyd, Sarah and Charles Boyd, John Abrams, and Cheryl Westbrook.

Dedicated friends and beta readers continue to make my writing better and remind me why sharing our stories matters. Thank you, Heidi Fettig Parton, Kim MacQueen, Jodie Baker, Lisa Werhan, Karen Cahalane, Jena Sujat, MaryAnne Morris, Doris Troy, and Matt Dube for your keen eyes and valuable feedback.

And to my publishing team at Vine Leaves Press, thank you for believing in this book: Jessica Bell, Amie McCracken, Melanie Faith, and my outstanding editor, Alexis Paige.

Excerpts previously appeared in similar forms in *Hippocampus Magazine, riverSedge Literary Journal, Write Angles Journal,* and *Entropy.*

Lyrics by David Berman appear courtesy of Bank Robber Music and Rough Trade Publishing.

Vine Leaves Press

Enjoyed this book?
Go to *vineleavespress.com* to find more.
Subscribe to our newsletter: